PERSPECTIVES ON

CUBA

AND ITS PEOPLE

by

Theodore A. Braun

Friendship Press, National Council of Churches
New York

Editorial Offices:
475 Riverside Drive, New York NY 10115

Distribution Offices:
P.O. Box 37844, Cincinnati, Ohio 45222-0844

Manufactured in the United States of America

Library of Congress Cataloging-in-Publication Data

Braun, Theodore A.
   Perspectives on Cuba and its people / by Theodore A. Braun.
      p.   cm
   Includes bibliographical references.
   ISBN 0-377-00326-3
   1. Cuba—History.   2. Christians—Cuba—History.   3. Christianity and international affairs.   I. Title.
   F1776.B78 1999
   972.91—dc21   98—54361
                                                                      CIP

CONTENTS

DEDICATION

"Any book worth the tree it still carries is a community enterprise," wrote Larry Rasmussen in *Earth Community, Earth Ethics*. This book, which I hope is "worth the tree it still carries," has been a broad community enterprise. It has sought to include the voices of many people—both Cubans and non-Cubans—involved in the past five centuries of the struggle of a people to live as subjects rather than objects of their history. For me it has been a great privilege to come to know many of the contemporary participants in this struggle that is important to all of us. This book is dedicated to them.

CONVERSATION WITH CASTRO

by Joan Brown Campbell, General Secretary
National Council of the Churches of Christ in the USA

O n a balmy summer evening in Havana, in June 1998, I, the rest of an NCC delegation, and three leaders of the Cuban Council of Churches dined at the "palace" with Castro, president of Cuba, and four of his highest officials. Surrounded by tropical trees, plants, and singing birds, we broke bread together and then continued talking for the next six hours. It was a remarkable and memorable experience.

With me were Rev. Dr. Clifton Kirkpatrick, Stated Clerk of the Presbyterian Church (U.S.A.); the Rt. Rev. Mckinley Young, Ecumenical Officer for the African Methodist Episcopal Church; Dr. Thom White Wolf Fassett, General Secretary, United Methodist Church Board of Church and Society; the Rev. Dr. Albert Pennybacker, NCC Director for Public Policy; the Rev. Oscar Bolioli, NCC/CWSW Director for Latin America and the Caribbean; Ms. Carol Fouke, NCC Director for News Services, and myself. Also present for the conversation were the President, Vice President, and General Secretary of the Cuban Council of Churches.

We talked nonstop. No topic was off limits. We discussed personal matters, politics, and national and international issues. Though in dress uniform for the occasion, Castro was relaxed, reflective, and, I believe, honest in his responses to our many questions. He listened carefully to the opinions we expressed.

Reflecting at length on the meaning of the historic visit to Cuba of Pope John Paul II, Castro was basically positive. He agreed that space for the churches to offer service and to bear witness had thereby been enhanced. It was moving to hear him describe lengthy personal conversations with the Holy Father. He mused about their apparent compatibility, yet he missed none of the pope's criticism of both the Cuban government and the American government.

The president reflected on the Holocaust, on the media (including the growing influx of pornography into Cuba through means such as the Internet), on the growth of prostitution, and, of course, on the embargo. There was little anger in his voice—only sadness. He thanked the NCC and its member churches for all the humanitarian aid we had brought over the years. He praised the Cuban Protestant churches and their support of the Cuban ideal that each citizen should have food, health care, and education.

On behalf of both the U.S. and Cuban Christians, I made four requests of Castro:

- That the Cuban churches be allowed to continue growing and witnessing to the love of Jesus Christ. *Castro affirmed their growth and praised the Protestant churches for ordaining native Cuban pastors.*
- That the Cuban churches be allowed to build new churches and refurbish older churches and that U.S. denominations be allowed to assist in the rebuilding process. *Castro agreed.*
- That the Cuban churches be allowed to increase their service to the Cuban people, especially service to the elderly, and to work with prostitutes and their families. *Castro said yes.*
- That the Cuban churches be given access to the air waves so their message might reach more people. *Castro quickly noted the complexity of responding favorably to this request but did not completely close the door.*

I felt that he heard our concerns and that he responded with candor. I pray that our sisters and brothers in Cuba feel that we presented their requests effectively and that their witness to the Cuban people continues to grow.

As I sat across the table from Fidel Castro that night, I was abundantly aware that he has been considered an enemy by the U.S. government for almost forty years, and I was struck anew by the unique role the church can play when nations fail to work well with one another. Despite our best efforts, people suffer—as they do today in Cuba—making it imperative that we in the churches speak truth in love, even to those our nation calls "enemy." I believe we were heard on that night in Havana.

The Cuban people are God's children, as are we all. We owe them our prayers, our understanding, our patience, and our support as they work out their own future. This book is intended to help us do our part.

"Encountering Cuba Again for the First Time"

T he island of Cuba lies just 90 miles south of the United States. Shaped like a 775-mile-long crocodile and home to 11 million people, it is similar in mass and population to the state of Pennsylvania. When Columbus landed there in 1492, he called it "the most beautiful land human eyes have seen," and the beauty of the country still makes a profound impact upon both residents and visitors.

From Cuba's earliest days, its neighbors to the north have had strong interest in this island. British colonial merchants incorporated it into their Triangle Trade of slaves, rum, and merchandise; early U.S. presidents desired to buy it from Spain; Confederate states hoped to annex it as a slave state: and several cities in the United States, such as Tampa and New York, became havens for Cuban exiles. When Cuba became a republic in 1902, it became a prime target for U.S. investment, exploitation, tutelage, and discipline. In 1959, however, when Cuba finally became an agent of its own history, alienation and blockade resulted. (The United States and the United Nations use the term *embargo*. Cubans use *blockade*. Both terms broadly mean a restriction on trade. The author prefers "blockade" because the United States is restricting not only itself but other countries from trading with Cuba.)

Since then, the United States has installed a trade, travel, and infor-mation blockade around the island and has engaged in a virtual war against Cuba, going so far as to deny its population access to shipments of food and medicine. U.S. citizens traveling to Cuba have been required to go indirectly via another country and to apply for a U.S. Treasury license to spend money there. Because of this barrier, many of us in the United

States know little about Cuba. Much of the information we have comes through either media reflecting the government's position or U.S. citizens and Cubans who feel most alienated from the Cuban historical process.

Those who are able to cross the information and travel blockade, however, soon discover a nation in process, constantly evolving, continually struggling—a Cuba that has moved on since the last time they encountered it. They meet a people of great warmth, resilience, resourcefulness, and creativity. And they soon perceive that present-day Cuba is neither heaven nor hell but somewhere in between, depending upon the location and perspective of the viewer.

This matter of location and perspective is a very important one, for we know now that there is no completely objective history. History is always written from a particular location and viewpoint, usually from the perspective of those in power. Howard Zinn, in his book *A People's History of the United States* (1980), has done much to sensitize us to the importance of viewing history from below—from the viewpoint of Indians, blacks, poor immigrants, women, and all those whose stories and perspectives have been left out of the official histories.

Because the indigenous inhabitants of Cuba left no written record, we cannot escape being dependent upon the observations and insights of those who did write, although we can give priority to those observers who we believe had the highest sensitivity and greatest insight. And when we come to written history, we discover that most of the chief actors on the Cuban stage and the recorders of its history, as everywhere in the world, have been men. The effort of the Cuban revolution to change this situation and reduce the high level of machismo has been one of the important priorities of that nation.

One's location can make a great difference in other ways. For instance, that fateful encounter between two cultures on October 28, 1492, can be viewed in two different ways: Columbus discovered the Taino people when he landed in Cuba, or the Taino people discovered Columbus on the shore when he landed. Either way this encounter of two worlds was not a benign one but an invasion, and from then on, Cuba's history was full of violence. On the five hundredth anniversary of Columbus' arrival in the Americas, various educational programs and resources did much to help North Americans re-read the past and re-think the role of Columbus.

Location has also been a critical factor in international relations. Over the past decades Cuba has been described by the United States as a "problem," and a number of U.S. presidents have promised to "solve the problem of Cuba." But to the people in Cuba, it was first Spain that was a "problem," and then the United States. It is this second immense problem that Cuba is still trying to solve today. This second problem also deeply concerns the United States' northern neighbor. Canada has never participated in the U.S. blockade, maintaining open travel and trade and friendly relations with Cuba. We will want to take a look at this witness and to see what kind of North American options and possibilities there are.

This book will try to be sensitive to both Cuba and Canada and not use the arrogant terms "America" or "American" when referring only to the United States. When José Martí, Cuba's national hero, spoke of America, he would invariably use two qualifying adjectives: "Our America" when referring to Latin or Spanish America, and the " Other America," when referring to the United States, or Anglo-Saxon America.

In an attempt to help readers encounter Cuba again for the first time, this book will give special attention to the role Christians have played in Cuban history, often on opposite sides of issues and conflicts. Most histories have overlooked or minimized this important ingredient in the story of Cuba. The church arrived in Cuba with Columbus on that fateful day in 1492, and from that moment on it was involved in continuing conflict over political, economic, ethical, and theological issues, both legitimizing oppression and inspiring revolution.

Several biblical themes provide a special lens for us as we look at the unfolding of Cuban history. One is Moses' project of prophetic criticism and action that Walter Brueggemann describes in his book *The Prophetic Imagination* (1978). In Egypt, Moses opposed Pharaoh's oppressive politics and economics and the royal religion that legitimized that system, countering it with politics, economics, and religion characterized by justice and compassion.

A second theme is the Jubilee motif in Leviticus 25 and Deuteronomy 15:1–15: the call to engage in faithful practice that includes a period of rest for the land, the liberation of slaves, and the cancellation of debts every fifty years.

A third is the project of prophetic criticism and action carried on by Jesus as he invited people into a new order of shalom (wholeness, peace). In contrast to the traditional social system based on the Temple in Jerusalem, which was hierarchical, exclusive, and ideologically oriented to the upper classes, Jesus formed an alternative community that was egalitarian and radically inclusive. His manifesto of liberation and Jubilee action is given in Luke 4:18–19 (confirmed when John's disciples come to him in Luke 7:18–23) and is further illustrated by his reaching out to women and Samaritans—even to the extent of being called a Samaritan by the Jewish leaders (John 8:48).

A fourth theme is found in Ephesians 2:14–16: Christ Jesus is described as our peace (shalom), who has broken down the dividing walls of hostility, creating in himself a new humanity and bringing about reconciliation.

In 1971 when speaking to Roman Catholics about the Cuban revolution, Fidel Castro said, "We have now arrived at the point not simply of coexistence between religion and revolution but for the best possible relationship. A Christian who understands Christ's words in their essence simply cannot be on the side of the exploiters, on the side of those who promote injustice, hunger, and misery."

In its essence, then, the Cuban revolution has something to do with sharing, with the distribution of goods and services, as Blase Bonpane points out in his book *Guerrillas of Peace* (1985). How these things are shared—who gets what and why—is a matter of politics, and of theology.

As we go further into these matters, we will be asking Cuba probing questions, and we, in turn, if we are attentive, will be questioned by Cuba. For as Cuba ceases to be an object of North American intervention and control and is allowed to become the subject of its own sovereignty and history making, it also becomes an important interlocutor for North Americans—challenging us to look anew at our own values, goals, actions, and faith. We have much to share with each other as God calls us to celebrate life and shalom together. Perhaps this is what it means most profoundly to be a neighbor.

CHAPTER 1

CUBA UNDER SPANISH RULE

Our first task in approaching another people, another culture, another religion, is to take off our shoes, for the place we are approaching is holy. Else we may find ourselves treading on [people's] dreams. More serious still, we may forget that God was here before our arrival.

We have, then, to ask what is the authentic religious content in [their] experience. We may, if we have asked humbly and respectfully, still reach the conclusion that our brothers [and sisters] have started from a false premise and reached a faulty conclusion. But we must not arrive at our judgment from outside their religious situation.

We have to try to sit when they sit, to enter sympathetically into the pains and griefs and joys of their history and see how those pains and griefs and joys have determined the premises of their argument. We have, in a word, to be "present" with them.

—John V. Taylor, *The Primal Vision*

THE INDIGENOUS PEOPLES AND THE ARRIVAL OF THE SPANISH

At the end of the fifteenth century, the largest of the three groups of indigenous people on the island of Cuba were the Tainos ("People of the Good"). They lived in thatched huts (*bohios*) and on their communal farms raised maize, potatoes, pineapples, and chili for the cooking pot, tobacco for smoking and healing purposes, and herbs for their medical properties. The open area in each village was used for assemblies, festivities and dancing, and a marketplace. Women were highly regarded, often serving as herbal doctors. The Tainos were known for their hospitality, pottery and other inventions, sports, poetry, and travel. They rarely engaged in fighting, except in defense against the raiding

Caribs. The Tainos believed in an invisible Supreme Being, Yocahu Vagua Maorcoti, who was identified with harvest and fruitfulness. Most families kept religious objects (*zenus*) made out of wood, stone, shell, and cotton in household shrines. They believed that after death their spirits went to a paradise called Coalbai.

On October 27, 1492, the Tainos saw a large ship approaching their island. The next day they discovered on their shore a group of Italian and Spanish sailors whose leader thought he had landed in India. They gave the strangers a warm welcome. In their brief visit the Europeans found no gold, but when they left, they took a number of Tainos with them.

After Columbus had returned to Spain, he described in a letter to one of his patrons, Raphael Sanchez, treasurer of Aragon, the people he had met:

> As soon . . . as they see that they are safe and have laid aside all fears, they are very simple and honest and exceedingly liberal with all they have; none of them refusing anything he may possess when he is asked for it, but, on the contrary, inviting us to ask them. They exhibit great love toward all others in preference to themselves. They also give objects of great value for trifles, and content themselves with very little or nothing in return. (Bigelow, "Discovering Columbus," in *Rethinking Columbus*, 1991, p. 7)

But he included an ominous note in his ship's log. "Should your majesties command it, all inhabitants could be taken away to Castile, or be made slaves on the island. With 50 men we could subjugate them all and make them do whatever we want."

In 1493 this sailor, explorer, and conquistador returned with seventeen ships and twelve thousand colonists to the six Caribbean islands he had discovered. It was then that the Tainos made several startling discoveries. The explorer was no innocuous visitor but had a specific agenda. He had been funded by the Spanish monarchs Ferdinard and Isabella, whose treasury was low and who were hoping to find a new route to the riches of Asia. His first priority was to find gold and then to extend the Christian faith. They discovered too that he had given them a new name, "Indians," and their island a new name, "Juana" (after Ferdinand and Isabella's daughter). Sometime later the name was changed to "Cuba," a word of Indian derivation. But most startling of all, they discovered that the world they knew had been reformulated and reordered by a man in Rome they had never met and never knew existed.

In the late fifteenth century, Spain and Portugal seemed bent on annexing as much of the world as their explorers and soldiers could reach. To avoid what seemed like inevitable conflict, in 1493 Pope Alexander VI issued the bull *Inter caeterae divinae*, which drew a line down the center of the Atlantic Ocean, assigning the western half (the Americas) to Spain and the eastern half (Africa and Asia) to Portugal. Then he issued a "Proclamation of the Conquistadors" to be read to the indigenous peoples of the Americas.

God the Lord has delegated to Peter and his successors all power over all people on the earth, so that all people must obey the successors of Peter.

Now one of these popes has made a gift of the newly discovered islands and countries in America and everything that they contain to the kings of Spain, so that, by virtue of this gift, their majesties are now kings and lords of these islands and of the continent. You are therefore required to recognize holy Church as mistress and ruler of the whole world and pay homage to the Spanish king as your new lord.

Otherwise, we shall, with God's help, proceed against you with violence and force you under the yoke of the Church and the king, treating you as rebellious vassals deserve to be treated. We shall take your property away from you and make your women and children slaves. At the same time, we solemnly declare that only you will be to blame for the bloodshed and the disaster that will overtake you. (Simons, *Cuba from Conquistador to Castro*, 1996, pp. 74–75)

When Columbus returned to the Caribbean, he did some further exploring around Cuba but then concentrated his efforts on the island of Hispaniola (now Haiti and the Dominican Republic). There he established his headquarters and unleashed a campaign of terror against its population in an effort to extract gold. As Hans Koning described it in his book *Columbus: His Enterprise* (1976):

Every man and woman, every boy or girl of fourteen or older, in the province of Cibao . . . had to collect gold for the Spaniards. As their measure, the Spaniards used . . . hawks' bells. Every three months, every Indian had to bring to one of the forts a hawk's bell filled with gold dust. The chiefs had to bring in about ten times that amount. In the other provinces of Hispaniola, twenty five pounds of spun cotton took the place of gold.

Copper tokens were manufactured, and when an Indian had brought his or her tribute to an armed post, he or she received such a token, stamped with the month, to be hung around the neck. With that they were safe for another three months while collecting more gold. Whoever was caught without a token was killed by having his or her hands cut off. . . .

There were no gold fields, thus, once the Indains had handed in whatever they still had in gold ornaments, their only hope was to work all day in the streams, washing out gold dust from the pebbles. It was an impossible task, but those Indians who tried to flee into the mountains were systematically hunted down with dogs and killed to set an example for the others to keep trying. . . .

During those two years . . . , an estimated one half of the entire population of Hispaniola was killed or killed themselves. (pp.185–86)

In 1512 Columbus appointed Diego Velázquez de Cuellar to complete the conquest of Cuba. Hatuey, a Guahaba chief in Hispaniola who had fled to Cuba with a group four hundred men, women, and children, tried to warn the Tainos of the impending danger. Following are his words as recorded by the Spanish priest Bartolomé de las Casas:

> The Spaniards are ready to invade this island, and you are not ignorant now of the ill-usage our friends and countrymen have met with at their hands and the cruelties they have committed. . . . They are now coming hither with design to inflict the same outrages and persecutions upon us. . . . they are a very wicked and cruel people. . . . these Europeans worship a very covetous sort of God, so that it is difficult to satisfy him; to perform the worship they render to this idol, they will exact immense treasures from us, and will . . . reduce us to a miserable state of slavery, or else put us to death. (Simons, *Cuba*, 1996, p.86)

Then, displaying a small basket of gold and jewels to the Tainos, Hatuey declared: " This is their Lord. This is what they serve. This is what they are after. . . . They invoke a seditious God of blood and gold, and we have, on our side, a just and wise God."

Despite his warning, he was unable to convince the Tainos of the need for a unified resistance. When Vélasquez arrived, the inhabitants tried fighting back but were not able to withstand the firearms of the conquistadors. Hatuey was captured and sentenced to death for resisting the Spaniards and for refusing to lead them to hidden gold.

Chief Hatuey was burned at the stake for heading an Indian insurrection against the Spanish conquerors. Soldiers and a friar look on.

Just before being burnt at the stake on February 15, 1512, Hatuey was urged by a priest, Juan de Tesin, to accept Christianity and be baptized before he died, so that he could go to heaven. Hatuey asked the priests and soldiers surrounding him whether they were going to heaven. They responded affirmatively. "If the Christians are going to heaven," the chief replied, "then I do not want to go to heaven. I do not wish ever again to meet such cruel and wicked people as Christians who kill and make slaves of Indians."

Velásquez took two years to conquer the island. During this time, the Spanish established seven settlements—Baracoa, Santiago de Cuba, Bayamo, Puerto Principe (Camagüey), Sancti Spíritus, Trinidad, and Havana— each with a central plaza and large cathedral. They also set up a completely new economic system, which spelt disaster for the Indians.

As Gustavo Gutierrez wrote in his book *Las Casas: In Search of the Poor of Jesus Christ* (1993),

The inhabitants of the islands . . . saw their world fall to pieces. Types of labor were imposed that they had never known. Military expeditions were undertaken to obtain their total submission. There were lethal food shortages. The natives were abused and harassed. New diseases were pandemic. Depopulation, social disorder, violent protests, and frequently even the disappearance of any desire to go on living increased dramatically. There was a totally new state of affairs for the islands. (p.21)

THE NEW COLONIAL ECONOMY

The word *economy*, from the Greek word *oikos* (house or household), has to do with how a household is managed—by whom and for whose benefit. *Ecology* is a similar term, derived from *oikos*, relating particularly to the environment. Both "economy" and "ecology" are profoundly political and theological matters, having to do with how we organize society and manage the earth as God's stewards. This section will look at how the Spanish replaced the Tainos' economy, politics, and theology. It will consider how this new economy developed over the four hundred years of Spanish rule and how, toward the end of this period, the United States achieved increasing influence and power over the Cuban scene.

Columbus and the other conquistadors (accompanied by priests to give their conquest religious legitimation) were sponsored by the Spanish Crown. When they discovered a new land, they would first plant a cross on the shore and then declare the land the property of King Ferdinard and Queen Isabella. (A similar process took place in North America during the English colonization. Land in Virginia was declared to be the property of King George III, who later sold 157 acres, including the Natural Bridge, to Thomas Jefferson for twenty shillings. The parcel was then resold over the years, which is why this natural wonder is still in private hands, costing a visitor $8.00 to see it.)

The *Encomienda* System and the Indians

The new economy that supported the conquistadors was the *encomienda* system. It consisted of large tracts of Crown land, along with their Indian inhabitants, distributed by Diego Columbus (son of Christopher and captain-general of Hispaniola) to loyal supporters of the Crown for their lifetime. On their new lands, the conquistadors raised cattle (for meat and leather), tobacco, and, beginning in 1503, sugar. They also dug gold mines, until the gold ran out, and built dockyards in Havana to supply, repair, and build ships for the Spanish convoys between Central America and Spain. Havana became an important port.

All these enterprises, for the benefit of the landholders and the Crown, depended on forced labor. The Indians were not technically slaves but conquered people who were required to give their labor as tribute. They were also expected to grow their own food and were supposed to be protected by the landholders. This system was rationalized and legitimated by the Europeans' belief that the Indians were inferior to Europeans. As beasts, savages, or at best, children, the Indians had to be educated and evangelized by their "civilized" Christian conquerors. The *encomienda* system was seen as providing a better opportunity for the Spanish to carry out their civilizing mission.

In fact the system was much abused. Indians were made to work very hard, and Spanish landowners allowed their cattle, pigs, goats, sheep, and horses to roam over the Indians' farm plots and grasslands, destroying their crops and destabilizing their communities. The result for the Indians was famine, malnutrition, and despair, increasingly leading to suicide. Epidemics raged through the Indian population in 1519 and 1530, killing thousands. It is estimated that there were about 112,000 Indians in 1492. By 1519, they had decreased to 19,000 and by 1531, to 7,000. By 1550, there were fewer than 3,000 left.

One of the beneficiaries of the *encomienda* system and also its most vigorous opponent was the landholder and priest Bartolomé de las Casas (see box). In books and sermons he denounced Spanish cruelty to the Indians and urged the ending of the *encomienda* system. Largely through his efforts, it was abolished in 1542 and Spain passed new laws to protect the Indians. But they came too late and were later so modified that they were of little help.

Apostle of the Indies

Bartolomé de las Casas (1474–1566) went with his father from Spain to Hispaniola in 1502. He became a landholder and later a Dominican priest and took part in the conquest of Cuba. For his services to the Crown he was granted land in Cuba. Although his skillful management of his farms and mines brought him great wealth in a short time, he also observed the widespread Spanish cruelty to the Tainos and a brutal massacre at Caonao. Experiencing a complete change of heart, he began to report on the dark side of the Spanish-Indian encounter—viewing history, as it were, from below. He graphically described the Spaniards' brutality: forcing Indians to carry the Spaniards on their backs or in hammocks so their masters would not have to walk in the hot sun, using Indians as meat for Spanish bloodhounds, and engaging in contests of mutilating and beheading Indians to test the sharpness of Spanish swords.

Las Casas released his own Indians from forced labor and told the conquistador Velázquez that he had decided to oppose the *encomienda* system, a decision Velázquez called "monstrous." Undeterred, las Casas did all he could through his prophetic sermons and other writings, notably his *History of the Indies,* to weaken the power of the landholders and win recognition and respect for the Indians. He even went to Spain to convince the Crown to make changes. He also traveled to Peru and to Guatemala in his efforts to protect the Indians. His sermons and books had great impact on his time. He was both respected and detested as the "Defender of the Indians."

Sugar and African Slaves

Private ownership of large ranches and plantations, which could be passed down to heirs, replaced the *encomienda* system. By 1700, tobacco and coffee had become the leading exports. By the early 1800s, a slave revolt in Saint Domingue (now Haiti, see below) and the wearing out of cane fields in English and French Caribbean colonies led to a sudden increase in world sugar prices. Sugar became Cuba's chief cash crop, with most of the profit going to the Spanish landowners or to Spain as taxes.

The number of sugar mills doubled. Since sugar requires large acreage, more and more land was cleared, from an estimated 1,700 acres in the late 1700s to an annual 3,500 acres in the 1820s and an annual 13,000 acres in the 1840s. In 1840 sugar was 60 percent of total exports;

in 1860 it was 74 percent. Cuba was rapidly moving into a single-crop economy.

A sugar plantation, consisting of vast cane fields and a central sugar mill to process the cane, required a great deal of hard labor, which was provided by black slaves. The first black slaves were imported from West Africa in 1522 to replace the Indians. By 1650, there were 5,000 slaves, by 1774, 44,000. As the importance of sugar grew, so did the importation of slaves. Between 1790 and 1820, 227,000 were brought in, and between the sugar boom years of 1821 and 1831, 600,000. By that time, the black and mulatto population outnumbered the white.

Slavery was already an ancient institution when it reached the New World. It had flourished under the Romans, who often enslaved European, African, or Asian peoples whom they had conquered. For many centuries it had received the blessing of the church. In the sixth century, Pope Gregory the Great had tens of thousands of slaves on the papal estates. The medieval theologian Thomas Aquinas defended the institution, agreeing with Aristotle that a slave was an "inspired tool of his master." In 1454 Pope Nicholas V blessed the practice of enslaving conquered peoples. In 1493 Pope Alexander VI gave his blessing to the conquistadors for the task of taking slaves. In 1548 Pope Paul III granted to all men, including the clergy, the right to keep slaves.

Slavery was also recognized by Spanish law. Unlike law in English colonies, Spanish law gave slaveholders some responsibilities to maintain and christianize their slaves, who could no longer be fed to the bloodhounds or used as targets for swordplay, as the Indians had been. The law also gave slaves rights to marry, buy and sell property, and buy their own or their children's freedom. But the laws were frequently ignored. Many slaves were usually allowed only four or five hours of sleep a night. On many plantations, slaves were expected to last no longer than seven years from date of purchase.

Although the church, allied very closely with Spanish landowners, continued to give its blessing to slavery, there were significant and courageous exceptions. Three outstanding clerics on the faculty of the San Carlos y San Ambrosio College and Seminary in Havana (José Agustín Caballero, Felix Varela y Morales, and José de la Luz) declared publicly in 1826 that " Slavery was in essence opposed to religion, nature, and indeed any sense of virtue," and that " The slave traders were criminals trafficking in human blood" (Kirk, *Between God and Party*, 1989, p. 76). These three were also strong supporters of Cuban independence from Spain (see below).

In 1842 the Spanish Crown revised the law to define more clearly the owners' obligations toward slaves. The first five articles of the law dealt with religious matters: 1. "Every slaveowner shall instruct [slaves] in the basic principles of the Roman Catholic Apostolic Religion." 2. These religious classes were to be given "at night time, after the day's work had been concluded." 3. Slaves could be used for a maximum of two hours on Sunday and then only to clean . . . 4. Slave owners were to ensure that, as slaves reached the appropriate ages, "the holy sacraments be administered to them." 5. Slaves must show "the necessary obedience to the constituted authorities, the obligatory reverence to priests, and respect for white settlers" (Kirk, *Between God and Party*, p. 17). Like earlier laws, these provisions were frequently ignored.

CUBA'S RELATIONS WITH SPAIN AND THE UNITED STATES

In 1762–1763, at the end of the Seven Years War, which pitted Britain against Spain, the British occupied Havana for eleven months. They increased the slave trade, opened up commerce with British colonies to the north, and introduced freemasonary, an international brotherhood inspired by the Enlightenment and opposed to the Roman Catholic Church. Spain reclaimed Havana in 1763, but by that time, the short British occupation had given Cubans a taste for more freedom in trade. Spanish landowners in Cuba had had enough of Spanish laws that required them to pay taxes to, and trade only with, Spain.

In 1776 Spain, in an effort to draw Cuban trade away from Britain, opened Cuban ports to direct trade with North American ports. Cuba exported sugar, coffee, molasses, and tobacco north and imported flour, lumber, iron, clothing, furniture, and wine from the United States. In 1796 there were 150 ships trading with Cuba; by 1852, the number had grown to 1,886.

Evan Golder

Morro lighthouse and fort were built by the Spanish to guard Havana harbor, a major port for ships sailing from the Spanish colonies to Spain.

Cuba also became part of the lucrative Triangle Trade. Ships loaded with rum and fabrics sailed from the United States or Europe to ports in West Africa, where they sold their goods and brought slaves from African and Arab traders. This human cargo was shipped across the Middle Passage of the Atlantic, under terrible conditions, to the West Indies, where the slaves were sold for huge profits. The shipowners or captains then bought raw materials such as sugar and cotton and sold them in the United States and Europe, where they were converted into rum and cloth, to be sold in West Africa. This profitable trade continued for more then two hundred years. Although Britain had given in to pressure from the abolitionists and ended the slave trade in 1807, Spain resisted such pressure.

In 1800 the Spanish Crown ended the law that large estates had to descend to heirs. That meant that plantations could be bought and sold on the open market, a significant move that initiated an active real estate market and also opened the way for the purchase and control of family-owned sugar plantations by companies and foreign interests to create huge *latifundia*.

As its trade with Cuba grew, the United States was especially concerned that the island, located at a strategic spot in the Caribbean, and having great commercial potential, not fall into the hands of a powerful foe. In 1783 John Adams, later to become U.S. president, wrote to the statesman Robert Livingston that Cuba was a natural extension of the American continent and that an American annexation of Cuba was indispensable to the continued safety of the United States. In 1805 President Thomas Jefferson declared that the prospect of war with Spain would not deter the United States from seizing Florida and the island of Cuba. In 1823 John Quincy Adams, who also became president, described Cuba as a ripening fruit that would inevitably fall into the lap of the United States. Its importance to our national interests, he said, was greater than that of any other foreign territory.

Several U.S. presidents offered to buy the island from Spain. In 1848 James Polk offered $100 million. In 1854 Franklin Pierce offered $130 million. In 1857 James Buchanan made a third offer. And in 1898 William McKinley offered $300 million. Each time, Spain refused to sell its lucrative colony. Many people in the Unites States, however, were not in favor of annexing Cuba. They opposed taking on responsibility for Cuba's debts, and they feared that converting a million Cuban blacks into U.S. citizens would intensify the slavery question in the United States.

Interest in the U.S. annexation of Cuba was not all one-sided. Many slaveholding planters in Cuba were in favor of it. Some of them initiated talks with the U.S. consul in 1810. Their interest continued throughout the nineteenth century, as they recognized that an economic relationship with the United States was already a fact of Cuban life. The United States was steadily penetrating the Cuban economy. Many Cuban handholders had taken out U.S. loans and were using machinery made in U.S. factories. Moreover, many plantations had been bought by U. S. businessmen. The first Cuban railroad had been built by a U.S. engineer in 1837. In 1844 a New Orleans company had installed gas lighting in Havana, and in 1849 a U.S. business had acquired the telegraph concession. By 1850, the United States accounted for a third of the island's trade, a higher percentage than Spain's. In 1888 nineteen U.S.-owned sugar refineries merged to form the American Sugar Refining Company, which received the bulk of Cuban raw sugar exported to the United States and supplied between 70 and 90 percent of the refined sugar sold there.

As Geoff Simons described that period in his book *Cuba: From Conquistador to Castro* (1996),

American merchants, bankers, industrialists and shipowners now dominated key sectors of the Cuban economy. Spanish and other foreign companies continued useful levels of trade with the island, but by now Cuba had been drawn inexorably into the dominant orbit of American commerce. The problems experienced by the Spanish in maintaining slavery and, after its abolition, in resourcing the moribund colonial system often served American interests.

After the Ten Years' War (1868–1878) [see below] the dislocated economy presented American entrepreneurs with fresh opportunities: merchants homed in on the sugar plantations, often acquiring dominant control; and other properties and real estate were offered to Americans at knock-down prices. Vultures from the northern colossus hovered over a desperate people struggling for independence. (pp.177–78)

Slave Revolts

There had been some slave revolts in Cuba in the seventeenth and eighteenth centuries, but they had been crushed. Cuban landowners were much afraid that the successful slave revolution led by Toussaint l'Ouverture in Saint Domingue (1791–1804) might be repeated by slaves in Cuba. Although the landowners wanted to import more slaves to work in the sugar plantations, many believed that a large influx of Africans would surely lead to revolution. As José Antonio Saco, a magazine editor, put it in 1848, " There is no country on earth where a revolutionary movement is more dangerous than in Cuba. . . . Under present circumstances, political revolution is necessarily accompanied by social revolution, and social revolution is the complete ruin of the Cuban race" (Jiménez, "The

19th Century Black Fear," *Afro Cuba: An Anthology of Cuban Writing on Race, Politics and Culture,* 1993, p. 39).

Such fears were not unfounded. Between 1812 and 1855 there were some dozen slave revolts, primarily among mine and plantation workers in the provinces of Matanzas and Oriente, in the northern and eastern parts of the island. They were speedily suppressed. Taking no chances, in 1825 the Spanish colonial government set up a Permanent Executive Military Commission to control every aspect of Cuban life. It censored the press, banned public meetings, and prohibited any discussion of slavery, political reform, or independence.

One revolt, however, was successful. A mutiny aboard the slave ship *Amistad,* off the coast in 1839, resulted in the Mende slaves taking control of the ship and ordering it back to Africa. The Cuban pilot, however, sailed east in the daytime but north at night. The ship ended up in Connecticut, where the slaves were imprisoned before being brought to trial. In prison they were befriended by Congregational abolitionists and Yale students, who taught them English. They were defended in a famous case before the U.S. Supreme Court by John Quincy Adams, who won their freedom.

Finally in 1853 the Spanish government, fearing U.S. intervention, directed the captain-general of Cuba to stop the slave trade. Although slave labor had become more costly than paid labor using machines, many slave owners denounced the decision, arguing that the "barbarous" Negroes would "submerge the white population, morality would collapse, and Christian civilization would perish." They called for the U.S. annexation of Cuba as the only way of preserving the slave system; white racists in the United States called for military intervention in Cuba to protect Christian values. The slave trade was effectively ended in 1864. Slavery itself was not declared illegal until 1879, when it was converted to "apprenticeship," and it lingered in practice till 1886. The owners received no compensation for their lost labor force, and the blacks received nothing with which to start a new life.

Meanwhile, between 1853 and 1874, landowners imported 125,000 indentured Chinese laborers from Canton to augment slave labor in the fields or as domestics. Thirteen percent died on the way over or soon after their arrival. Because of the poor working conditions and low pay (four pesos a month), most left Cuba after their eight-year contract expired. Another 39,000 arrived during the 1920s. Most of those who remained married Cuban women.

WARS OF INDEPENDENCE

Many Cubans, resenting the increasingly harsh economic and political control of Spain, joined the growing rebellion. In 1868 a Spanish planter and slaveowner, Carlos Manuel de Céspedes, accompanied by a group of Oriente planters, declared independence. Freeing his slaves and leaving his house at Yara (the town of Chief Hatuey), he burned his own sugar mill and with 146 fellow patriots, raised the cry of "Independence or death!" the famous *Grito de Yara* (Cry of Yara). Soon joined by twelve thousand men, Céspedes and his small army captured Bayamo and Holguín.

Peasants, slaves, and freed men joined the rebels as they swept through eastern Cuba. A republic was proclaimed in 1869 with Céspedes as president, although there was no single mind on the common issue of slavery. The Spanish retaliated by sending a 40,000-man army and a Volunteer Corps of bloodthirsty adventurers. Eventually 100,000 Spanish soldiers were fighting, forcing civilians into prison camps, conducting mass executions, plundering houses, and regaining rebel territory.

New rebel leaders, the Dominican exile Maximo Gómez and the Cuban mulatto Antonio Maceo (the Bronze Titan), instituted guerrilla warfare, hoping to carry the war into the western provinces, but the rebels were divided and the wealthier western planters opposed the abolition of slavery. Céspedes, who wanted gradual emancipation, was deposed in 1873 and killed in ambush the next year. Finally in 1878 hostilities came to an end with the signing of the pact of Zanjón, although it was rejected by General Maceo because it did not call for the abolition of slavery or the independence of Cuba.

Ten years of fighting in this first War of Independence (1868–1878) resulted in the loss of 200,000 Spanish lives and 50,000 Cuban rebel lives and the ruin of many sugar plantations, destroying the power of the old landed aristocracy. It had not resolved tensions between Spain and the supporters of Cuban independence. Spain also added its cost of war, $300 million, to the Cuban debt. Spain refused all Cuban requests for reform, inspired by the patriotic writings of José Martí, a poet and journalist living in exile (see box). Meanwhile, U.S. businessmen bought up much property from Cubans ruined by the war. A U.S. tariff law in 1894 severely restricted exports of sugar to the United States, producing an economic crisis. This situation exploded in the Second War of Independence (1895–1898).

"Mentor of the Cuban Nation"

Probably the most influential Cuban in the four centuries of colonial rule was José Martí (1853–1895). Lawyer, poet, essayist, newspaper publisher, orator, political organizer, political prisoner, professor, philosopher, ambassador, advocate of the poor, and keen interpreter of his time, José Martí has been called the Mentor of the Cuban Nation, the Cuban Apostle, and the Keystone of the Cuban Identity. Already devoted to the cause of Cuban independence, he was sentenced as a teenager to prison and hard labor for some anti-Spanish writing, and then exiled.

Martí studied law in Madrid, lived in Mexico, taught language and philosophy in Guatemala, returned to Cuba, and was again arrested and deported. Thus time he moved to New York, where he gave speeches, wrote articles and tracts, and began an intensive effort to unify and organize the Cuban people in anticipation of an independent, liberal nation. He also raised funds to buy arms for the coming struggle against Spain.

At first Martí was greatly enamored of life in the United States. But the longer he lived there, the more disturbed he was by the materialism of the developing capitalist culture he saw everywhere. "Via the 'cult of wealth,' big business had succeeded in corrupting 'the courts, the legisla-

José Martí, Cuban patriot in the Second War of Independence, appears in painting and sculpture and on the one-peso note.

tures, the church, and the press' to create 'the most shameful of oligarchies,' " he wrote. He concluded that powerful business interests had gained control of both parties. He also believed that the possibility of annexation to the United States was the greatest threat to Cuba's independence.

The goal of the revolution, as Martí saw it, was to build a republic *con todos y para el bien de todos* (with all and for the good of all). He made a special effort to applaud the contributions of blacks to the revolutionary struggle and to include them in his movement. He also recognized that freedom would come at a great cost: "to many generations of slaves must follow one generation of martyrs."

As John Kirk points out in his book *José Martí: Mentor of the Cuban Nation* (1983), Martí envisioned a complete reshaping of the social structure, of political life, and of economic organization. He planned a classless and "colorless" state in which for the first time in Cuban history all citizens would be allowed equal privileges. A determined attempt would be made to provide full employment for all Cuban workers, and all citizens would be able to receive a basic education. In return for the many concrete social advantages that would be available to the people as a whole, Martí hoped to convince his fellow Cubans of the validity of a reinvigorated work ethic and of the essential dignity of human toil. He felt that the Roman Catholic Church should be stripped of its political power and prevented from teaching religion in the schools. To this end he formed the Revolutionary Cuban Party, in the hope that a single party would provide a strong defense in Cuba against the divisive efforts of the northern giant.

At the beginning of the Second War of Independence in 1895, Martí returned to Cuba to participate in the struggle. The day before he was killed in the war's first battle, he wrote to a friend in Mexico,

It is my duty—inasmuch as I realize it and have the spirit to fulfill it—to prevent, by the independence of Cuba, the United States from spreading over the West Indies and falling, with that added weight, upon other lands of our America. All I have done up to now, and shall do hereafter, is to that end. . . . I have lived inside the monster and know its entrails—and my weapon is only the slingshot of David. (Martí, *Inside the Monster*, 1975, front matter)

Kirk makes a very interesting point: Martí has been adopted as a political symbol and hero by Cubans in two quite contrasting ways—one, reflecting a traditional pre-revolutionary interpretation of Martí (continued today in the writings of Cuban exiles in the United States), the second, reflecting a newer interpretation of Martí as revolutionary.

The first way focuses on the moral qualities of Martí's life as a saint, a great and selfless Cuban, and an apolitical giant; the second focuses on his radical social and political writings, his vocation as a revolutionary, and his plans for a liberated Cuba. The first lifts up passages in Martí's writings that were appreciative of U.S. leaders and institutions, while the second lifts up passages that criticize U.S. arrogance, imperialism, consumerism, classism, and racism, and describes life lived the "belly of the beast." The first sees Martí as legitimizing the view from above. That is why his name has been chosen for interventionist, counterrevolutionary media such as TV Martí and Radio Martí. The second sees him as justifying the view from below. That is why when one travels through Cuba, one finds busts of Martí everywhere—in the front yards of houses, in schools, workplaces, and even churches. One bears his saying that "All people can be divided into groups: those who love and build, and those who hate and destroy."

Spanish troops and Cuban troops ravaged the country. In 1898 the unified Cuban forces, led by Generals Gómez and Maceo and augmented by black slaves and freed men, were coming close to victory. The closer they came, the more anxious the United States became about the emergence of a new power in the Caribbean. For years the public had been stirred up by "yellow journalism," which used racist stereotypes to depict Cubans and other Latin Americans as inferior and in need of U.S. intervention and direction. William Randolph Hearst's personal credo was, "Newspapers form and express public opinion. They suggest and control legislation. They declare wars." And so when his *Journal* correspondent in Cuba in 1897 complained, " There will be no war," Hearst cabled back, "Please remain. You furnish the pictures and I'll furnish the war."

On February 15, 1898, the U.S. battleship *Maine*, anchored in Havana harbor, blew up, killing 260 men. The Spanish inquiry concluded that the explosion was an internal one, while the U.S. investigation concluded that it was an external one caused by a mine. (A special U.S. investigation in 1976 under the direction of Rear Admiral Hyman G. Rickover decided that the evidence was consistent with "an internal explosion alone"—most likely from "heat from a fire in the coal bunker adjacent to the 6-inch reserve magazine.") Hearst's *Journal* headlined *"THE WARSHIP MAINE WAS SPLIT IN TWO BY AN ENEMY'S SECRET INFERNAL MACHINE"* and began to whip up war fever in the United States. By April 19, the United States had joined the war in Cuba, much to the displeasure of the Cuban rebels. Nevertheless, U.S. forces landed at sites recommended by the rebels and enjoyed their protection. Cuban General Calixto García hoped at least that the U.S. soldiers would come to know and respect the Cubans and that the people in the United States would be convinced that the Cubans were able to govern themselves.

Cuban forces helped contain Spanish soldiers at Guantánamo and Holguín, and then used García's plans for the battle of Santiago de Cuba. U.S. forces stormed two small hills on the edge of the city (Kettle and San Juan), laid siege to the city, sank the small Spanish fleet in the harbor, and then accepted the surrender of the Spanish general in Santiago. At the end of four months, the war was over. U.S. Secretary of State John Hay described the conflict: "It has been a splendid little war; begun with the highest motives, carried on with magnificent intelligence and spirit favored by that fortune which loves the brave."

What the victorious Cubans did not realize was that a new order had been formulated for their world. General García and his men were not allowed by the U.S. forces to participate in the victory celebrations and the military parade held in Santiago and were excluded from all the other cities. Nor were Cubans present when the war in Cuba officially ended on August 12, 1898, with representatives of the United States and Spain signing a preliminary protocol. Spain agreed to give up sovereignty over Cuba and to evacuate the island, but the United States refused to give the Cuban leadership any political status.

On October 1 the peace conference opened in Paris without the Cubans. Spain suggested that the United States might assume sovereignty over Cuba, including the $400 million Cuban debt. The United States refused this annexation option, preferring one that would maximize commercial opportunities and control with minimum cost. It was soon apparent that the United States had in mind a military administration for a starter. So ended four hundred years of Spanish political and economic rule.

COLONIAL WAY OF LIFE

Most of the Spanish who came to Cuba, as to other parts of the New World, were in search of as much wealth as possible. They appropriated the island's mineral, land, and human resources, turning them into commodities owned by the Crown or, later, by private individuals or corporations. The value of these commodities was determined by the amount of profit they could produce for their owners and for taxes to the Crown. Sugar plantations using African slave labor became the main source of profit, as described above.

The plantation system was reflected in the hierarchical structure of Spanish colonial society, unlike the egalitarian society of the Tainos. At the top of the colonial social pyramid was the Spanish-born aristocracy: large landowners, the captain-general, and other Crown officers, who ran the

Spanish-born landowners and Crown officers enjoyed luxurious houses, such as this Havana mansion with its elaborate wrought iron gate.

government; the clergy, who controlled the church and education and provided legitimacy for the government; and the military, who guaranteed peace and order as defined by the aristocracy. Below the Spanish-born elite came the Criolla (Creoles), offspring of Spaniards born in Cuba. They held smaller amounts of the land and lesser government posts. Below them were people of mixed race (mulattos), then free blacks, and at the bottom black slaves.

The plantation system and the social pyramid it supported provided a comfortable, gracious life for those at the top. Some of them helped their dependents with jobs, money, and education. Many were indifferent. Conditions for the vast majority at the bottom were chiefly poverty and neglect. Nevertheless, there was room for music and dance and creativity and a marvelous ability to do a lot with a little.

Weaknesses in Society

Colonial Cuban society, based as it was on sugar and slavery, had certain inherent weaknesses. One was the fact that despite the Spanish claim to a "civilizing" and "Christianizing" mission, social relations were shaped by preoccupation with maintaining racial purity (at the top level) and gaining economic profit. These values imparted a demeaning, even dehumanizing dynamic that in the long run could only lead to social distintegration.

A second weakness was economic dependence on one crop. By concentrating on sugar, the Spanish colonists neglected to develop other agriculture, preferring to import the foodstuffs they needed. They also chose to export sugar rather than develop domestic industries, which in any event were forbidden by Spain. The value of this cash crop depended on prices in the world sugar market. When prices were up. Cuban growers flourished; when prices were down, they had to go out seeking for loans.

Thus colonial Cuba, like other Spanish colonies, was a client state on the periphery of the Spanish empire. Its function was to feed the metropolitan center, Spain, to which it was also oriented socially, politically, and psychologically. Later (see below), as the power of the United States began to supplant that of Spain, the island became increasingly integrated into the newly expanding U.S. empire, relating to the United States as a new metropolitan center. In both situations, however, Cuba's raison d'être remained the same—to serve as a segment of the "open veins of Latin America," an economic reality described by the Uruguayan author Eduardo Galeano in a book by that name.

A third weakness was the rigidity of the social hierarchy, which hindered the ability of the Spanish to cope with change and modernization. It was reinforced by a pervasive sense of fear and anxiety among the upper levels of the pyramid, uneasy about the possibility of rebellion from below. A number of slaves who bought or were given their freedom were able to move up the pyramid by entering service and craft occupations as tailors, shoemakers, carpenters, chauffeurs, cooks, laundresses, seamstresses, and cigar-makers—especially in Havana. But that gradual upward mobility was not enough to dispel fear of violence on the part of the elite.

By the end of the nineteenth century, as a result of two wars and economic pressure, the old landed aristocracy had virtually lost its control of the island's wealth. U.S. investors had taken control of the sugar economy and had penetrated other industries. To these new rich, Havana still offered the appearance of the old-time prosperity and pleasure—fine, pillared houses and gardens, bullfights, cockfights, gambling casinos, houses of prostitution, carnivals, masked balls, Sunday promenades by the sea, shops and cafés filled with foreign goods and delicacies, and theaters and concerts halls offering foreign entertainment. Always around the edges of the "prosperity," however, were the beggars, the thousands of unemployed who could find no work in the "dead season" (the eight months when the sugar plantations had no work to be done), and the sick and old.

Religious Life and Education

Throughout the centuries of Spanish rule, religious and educational life was dominated by the Roman Catholic Church. Protestantism, known as Evangelicalism in Cuba, was on the fringes of society, and Santeria was a popular underground movement.

Catholicism. The Roman Catholic Church was closely allied to the government and the aristocracy. Its cathedrals were in the cities, usually on the main plaza near the governor's palace and government offices. Most churches were also in cities, where the upper and middle classes tended to live. The church's income consisted of a government subsidy and fees charged for baptisms, weddings, and funerals. Most of the priests and members of religious orders came from Spain. The church appealed chiefly to women and was often their major interest outside the family, since upper-class women usually did not work. Most Cuban

The Cathedral of Havana, in the baroque style, was the grandest of the Roman Catholic churches that dominated the main plazas of Cuban cities.

men paid little attention to its teachings. Indeed many priests, who received no salary, lived with their housekeepers or mistresses.

The church's close ties to the government and the aristocracy were especially obvious in the early nineteenth century when a number of slave rebellions broke out. In response on April 8, 1826, the government issued a special decree that outlawed the importation of any book that opposed the church or the rights of the Crown or that justified rebellion of subjects of the king.

The church maintained schools, hospitals, clinics, and orphanages, but these were mainly in the cities and usually charged a fee. Thus both geographically and economically they were out of reach of the rural poor.

There were also some schools run by the state. Most of them were primary schools taught by teachers who had very little education themselves. They also charged a fee, and students had to buy uniforms and books. In 1820 perhaps 10 percent of free children went to church or public schools. No slave children did. In the 1890s about 20 percent of all school-age children went to public schools, about 15 percent to church or other private schools. Families who could afford it sent their children to school in Spain. The rest had no formal education. The University of Havana, founded in 1721, was open only to upper-class men.

Santeria. A number of various African religions were brought by slaves to the New World. Officially the Roman Catholic Church condemned all

24

these faiths as witchcraft, and Spanish slave owners forbade their slaves to practice the rituals; as a result, these religions had to be carried on secretly or be disguised by identification with Catholic saints. Eventually popular religions became a syncretistic blend of African and Catholic elements. The best-known was Santeria, which arrived with the Yoruba people. It is a monotheistic religion whose God, Olodumare, is seen as the creator of the universe. Humanity's personal God—an aspect of Olodumare—is Olofi. God's power or energy (*ashe*) is mediated through *orishas*, spirits who personify various natural forces or human interests. The ceremonies, reflecting African roots, make use of ritual music, dance, and sacrifices. Four basic ingredients are involved—water, herbs, cowrie shells, and stones—plus offerings to the *orishas* such as fruits, foods, and animals. The ceremonies, often including divination and trances, seek to bring the worshiper into harmony with God's creative force and to eliminate negative influences. They also seek to please the *orishas*, who may then be called upon to help the supplicant with the problems of daily life. Practitioners of Santeria are called *santeros* or *santeras* (devoted to the saints).

It is fascinating to try to deduce why certain *orishas* came to be identified with certain saints. Here are some of the identifications.

Oggun (representing work, brute force, raw energy, arguments, war) with St. Peter (head of the church)

Orunla (representing wisdom, patience, holy divination, herbal knowledge) with St. Francis of Assisi

Babalú-Ayé (representing cure of illness, compassion for those with broken or missing limbs, beggars) with St. Lazarus (a beggar in Luke 16:20)

Changó (representing fire, thunder, lightning, passion, virility, raw power) with St. Barbara (Changó was able to escape from enemies waiting for him outside his doorway by dressing as a woman.)

Obatalá (representing purity) with Our Lady of Mercy

Yemayá (representing the sea, life, sustenance) with Our Lady of the Regla

Elegguá (representing fate, justice, healing, divination) with St. Anthony of Padua (a great doctor of the Catholic Church, known for his knowledge of the Bible)

Santeria was scorned by Spanish governmental and church officials, but the power of the *orishas* gave the slaves a counter to the power of the oppressive society, and Santeria ritual in homes and sacred places offered them an alternative to the cathedral ritual of the empire. It formed a bond that tied the black population both to their past and to a future of hope.

Protestantism. Evangelicalism was brought to Cuba during the 1800s by pastors and by lay people who frequently traveled back and forth between the United States and Cuba, either to find work in the Cuban communities (such as in the tobacco factories in Tampa and Key West), or safety after participating in various rebellions and political opposition in Cuba. They began to preach and to open schools, which, like Catholic bodies, were principally in the cities.

In 1883 Dr. Alberto J. Diaz founded the Baptist work in Cuba, establishing ties with the Southern Baptist Church. The Methodist work in Cuba was founded in Guanabacoa by Rev. Enrique B. Someillan. The work of the Episcopal Church was started in Matanzas by Rev. Pedro Duarte. Presbyterian evangelism began through the efforts of a tobacco worker, Evaristo P. Collazo. Formerly a lay leader in the Episcopal Church, he started a preaching center, and his wife, Magdalena, opened a school for girls in their house in Havana. They later extended their work to Santa Clara. They formed ties with the Southern Presbyterian Church and, when that church left Cuba, with the Northern Presbyterian Church. Collazo was ordained a Presbyterian pastor in 1890.

One of the early problems these Evangelical church founders faced as they reached out for new members was the need to open cemeteries for Protestants. Roman Catholic ecclesiastical law did not permit the burial of "heretics," and the new converts feared that once they publicly accepted the faith of the Evangelicals, they would no longer have a place to be buried. The Baptists were able to obtain land in Havana for Protestant burials, and the Presbyterians, similar land in Santa Clara.

Another problem was the outspoken opposition of the Roman Catholic priests and sisters to Protestant evangelistic and educational work. A letter written by Collazo to a missionary in Mexico on Sept. 2, 1891, suggests that perhaps in back of the priests' anxiety was a recognition that the Cuban population was less than nominally Catholic: "Near this city there are many towns where years go by and no one says anything about the existence of God, because the priests do not bother about anything except financial business, and . . . to marry a couple or bury the dead they ask whatever they feel like without paying respect to the fixed fees or to the misery of the people."

One of the strengths of the early Evangelical mission effort was its spirit of ecumenical solidarity and cooperation. The first ecumenical gathering of Evangelical pastors on the island took place in Santa Clara on March 26, 1891, with one Episcopalian pastor, two Methodists, and two Presbyterians present. In 1895 Collazo, Someillan, Diaz, and Duarte all took active patriotic roles in the Second War for Cuban Independence, as part of José Martí's Cuban Revolutionary Party and the Mambisi forces.

By the end of the 1800s, there were missionaries in Cuba representing the Northern Baptist Church, Southern Baptist Church, Congregational Church, Disciples of Christ, Episcopal Church, Southern Methodist

Church, Northern Presbyterian Church, Southern Presbyterian Church, and the Society of Friends.

Anarcho-syndicalism. An influential movement among those who were not religiously minded was anarcho-syndicalism. In the 1880s Spanish anarcho-syndicalists came as exiles to Cuba bringing with them the conviction that the working class must try to build a new world without the imperfect institutional structures that supported exploitation and injustice. Their goals included the abolition of classes; the political, economic, and social equality of both sexes; and the conversion of the land, the instruments of labor, and all other property (except personal possessions) into the collective property of the whole society. They soon were providing important leadership in the unions in the maritime, railway, restaurant, and tobacco industries. They started a workers' club, published a newspaper, and made a great impact upon the Cuban labor movement. At the same time they brought down upon themselves the opposition of the conservative government, which imprisoned and deported their leaders. But by then, their ideas had taken root in the revolutionary soil of Cuba.

Questions for Reflection

1. In what ways could the Tainos be called responsible stewards of Cuba and of the integrity of creation?
2. To whom does land rightly belong in terms of ownership or stewardship? How are ownership rights originally established? Consider the difference between the indigenous people's view that land is sacred and to be protected for future generations and the European view that it can be privately owned and exploited. What is your reaction to the privatization of such natural resources as the Natural Bridge in Virginia?
3. What is the difference between viewing human beings as the objects of other people's history and viewing them as subjects of their own history? Are the two views exclusive?
4. Would you say that Bartolomé de las Casa's conversion made him more spiritually aware? Explain.
5. The world of the Spaniards seemed so different from the world of the Tainos that the Spanish sense of cultural superiority determined the whole form of colonial society. How could this situation have been changed or prevented?
6. What are the contrasting ways in which different groups of Cubans view José Martí? What similarities can you see between those views and the contrasting views that Christians have of the Bible? How does the position of the viewer affect his or her view?

Chapter 2

Cuba Under U.S. Domination

The four-year struggle for independence from Spain had taken a tremendous toll. Hundreds of thousands of Cubans perished; fields were burned; livestock was scattered; houses, bridges, roads, sugar mills, and railways were in ruins; mines were closed; commerce and manufacturing were at a standstill; unemployment was rampant. But the worst part came at the end when the Cubans discovered that their war for liberation had been transformed at the last moment into a U.S. conquest. Even their name for the struggle, the Second War for Independence, had been taken from them when the United States gave the conflict a new official name, the Spanish-American War.

U.S. Economic Influence

The name change was more than cosmetic. The United States had taken from Cubans the power to direct their own reconstruction and regeneration—to be the agents of their own history. The United States, in taking control of the Cuban government, had appropriated the mechanisms for policy formation, revenue collection, disbursement of public funds, and enforcement of law and order.

When the peace treaty between the United States and Spain was signed in Paris in October 1898, President William McKinley announced that the United States had authority over Cuba through "the law of belligerent right over conquered territory." He then appointed General John R. Brooke as the first U.S. military governor of Cuba, and under him six provincial governors of high military rank. General Brooke promptly issued a proclamation to the Cuban people: "The object of the present Government is to give protection to the people, [to provide] security to person and property, to restore confidence, to encourage the people to resume the pursuits of peace, to build up waste plantations, to resume commercial traffic, and to afford full protection in the exercise of all civil and religious rights."

It sounded benevolent, but behind it was a highly charged political situation. In Cuba there was a strong populist-nationalist element that favored independence and was angry that it had been denied. Among the Creole planters and other upper-class Cubans, however, there was still hope for annexation by the United States. Similarly many people in the United States opposed an independent Cuba and supported annexation.

The situation was further complicated by an amendment that Senator Henry M. Teller had added to a joint resolution before Congress in 1898 authorizing McKinley to go to war to end Spanish sovereignty over Cuba. The Teller Amendment stated: "The United States hereby disclaims any disposition or intention to exercise sovereignty, jurisdiction, or control over said Island except for the pacification thereof, and asserts its determination, when that is accomplished, to leave the government and control of the Island to its people."

Many people in the United States saw "pacification" as one of the most important purposes of the occupation—i.e., pacifying Cuba's independence movement and making sure that the reins of government were left in "responsible" hands. All across the United States there was growing anxiety about what would happen when the U.S. occupation ended. To justify this anxiety there was a concerted effort in the U.S. media to portray the Cubans as unready for self-government. Various journalists maintained: "Cubans are not inspired by the love of liberty but by the love of looting." "Cubans are possessed by the sole desire to murder and pillage." "If we are to save Cuba, we must hold it. If we leave it to Cubans, we give it over to a reign of terror—to the machete and the torch, to insurrection and assassination."

The military officials were equally condemnatory. "Self-government! Why those people are no more fit for self-government than gunpowder is for hell" (General William R. Shafter). "The insurgents are a lot of degenerates, absolutely devoid of honor or gratitude. They are no more capable of self-government than the savages of Africa" (General Samuel B. M. Young). "The Cubans are utterly irresponsible, partly savage, and have no idea of what good government means" (Major Alexander Brodie). "The Cubans are stupid, given to lying and doing all things in the wrong way. . . . Under our supervision, and with firm and honest care for the future, the people of Cuba may become a useful race and credit to the world, but to attempt to set them afloat as a nation, during this generation, would be a great mistake" (Major George M. Barbour).

Such views as these were not the exception. Cuba and other Caribbean and Central American countries were commonly pictured by editorial cartoonists in the United States in the form of children, primarily as black children. Such images called attention to their "immaturity," while the United States was assigned parental or guardian roles. They also played especially upon the widespread racism in the United States. As John J. Johnson wrote in his book *Latin America in Caricature* (1980),

In *Latin America in Caricature* by John J. Johnson, University of Texas Press, 1980.

"Uncle Sam: 'I'll give you one teaspoonful, Cuby. More of it might make you sick.' " This cartoon by William "Billy" Ireland (?) in the *Columbus* (Ohio) *Dispatch* of 1902 was typical of the United States' patronizing attitude to the newly independent Cuba.

The artists left very little to the imagination as they randomly selected from the long list of physical, oral, and social caricatures with which a prejudiced public could quickly relate.

The republics were lampooned variously as cheerful, improvident, carefree Blacks, meant to recall the myth of the "happy and content bondsman" or the popular minstrel of an earlier age. They became unintelligent, lazy, dozing people with a consuming appetite for cigars and watermelons or gunslinging, razor-wielding rowdies. And if words were put in their mouths, those words were almost always in southern Black dialect.

In brief, a black face and foreign dialect symbolically transformed Latin America into a stereotype that paralleled the condition of, and evoked from prejudiced White American society the same responses as [to], Blacks in the United States at a time when the prevailing ethic was "keep them in their place." (p.150)

In 1899 General Leonard Wood, who replaced Brooke as U.S. military governor, began immediately to facilitate further U.S. economic penetration of the island. He granted 218 tax-exempt mining concessions to foreign (mostly U.S.) companies and opened the doors to U.S. corporations, land companies and speculators, and individuals, who arrived by the shipload. The war-ravaged island, lacking capital or the means to generate it, seemed indeed like a ripe plum ready for the picking, and U.S. entrepreneurs with money and equipment moved in to take full advantage.

By 1905, thirteen thousand U.S. citizens had acquired title to land in Cuba; an estimated 60 percent of all rural property on the island was owned by U.S. corporations and individuals. In 1905, twenty-nine sugar mills were already owned by U.S. businessmen. U.S. corporations obtained concessions controlling gas, electric, and telephone services and entered the banking business.

Wood was not willing to grant universal suffrage to the Cuban people. In a letter to President McKinley, he commented that people without property were "a social element unworthy to be counted upon for collective purposes. . . . The people here, Mr. President, know that they are not ready for self-government and those who are honest make no attempt to disguise the fact . . . *we are dealing with a race that has been steadily going downhill for a hundred years*" (italics in the original).

Anxious to protect U.S. investment against the uncertainties that would come with the end of the occupation, the U.S. Congress in early 1901 passed an amendment to the Army appropriations bill that had been drafted by Senator Orville Platt. When McKinley signed the bill on March 2, this Platt Amendment became law. It permitted the United States to intervene at any time to protect life, liberty, and property; it gave the United States the right to review and approve all treaties and loan agreements between Cuba and other countries; and it required Cuba to sell or lease naval stations to the United States.

The Cubans were outraged. A cartoon in the Cuban newspaper *La Discusion* on Good Friday, April 2, showed a crucified Cuba between two thieves, Wood and McKinley, with a spear-holding Senator Platt nearby. The United States, however, insisted that it would not withdraw from Cuba unless this amendment were incorporated as an appendix to the new Cuban Constitution being drafted. On May 28 after much deliberation, the Cuban Constitutional Convention accepted the addition of the Platt Amendment by a vote to 15 to 14.

When the first elections were held, in December 1901, Afro-Cubans, women, and those with less than $250 worth of assets were excluded from voting. Tomás Estrada Palma, who had been one of the leaders of the Cuban Revolutionary Party founded by Martí but had spent the past twenty-two years in the United States, was elected president. But Estrada turned out to be quite different from Martí. Having absorbed a U.S. mentality, he became the first of a series of pliant presidents who helped to increase the island's subservience to its new metropolitan center.

After Estrada took office on May 20, 1902, ending the U.S. occupation, the United States took two additional steps to tighten its control over the island. First, in March 1903, it signed a commercial reciprocity treaty by which Cuba received lower tariff rates for selected exports in return for reducing duties on certain U.S. imports. This had the effect of encouraging Cuban dependency on sugar and discouraging economic diversification. Second, on May 22, the United States signed a treaty with Cuba, which incorporated the Platt Amendment. It specified two locations for U.S. naval stations—Guantánamo Bay and Honda Bays. Cuba had to turn over Guantánamo Bay to the United States on a perpetual lease for $2,000 a year in gold. In 1912 the United States extended the boundaries of Guantánamo in exchange for giving up the Honda Bays location. The naval base was then used to help control the Caribbean and the route to the Panama Canal and also for subsequent U.S. invasions of the Dominican Republic, Haiti, Nicaragua, Mexico, and Panama.

For the first half of the twentieth century, the central fact of the Cuban economy was its domination by U.S. monopolies. Cuba's dependency could be seen in almost every area of its economy—sugar, manufacturing, transportation, electricity, oil, and tourism. Although U.S.-owned sugar mills accounted for only 15 percent of Cuban sugar production in 1906, by 1920 they accounted for almost 50 percent and by 1929, 75 percent. By 1926, half of all Cuban sugar was being processed in the United States by seven U.S. companies, notably the giant American Sugar Refining Company. Another U.S. giant, the Tobacco Trust, controlled 90 percent of the export trade of Havana cigars. U.S. banks held one-fourth of all the bank deposits in Cuba, including $2.5 million in mortgages. U.S. investments increased eightfold between 1902 and 1929. By 1911, total U.S. investment in Cuba had passed $200 million. By 1929, the total reached more than $1.5 billion, almost 30 percent of U.S. investments in all Latin America.

The skewed nature of the relationship, however, could be seen in the export-import picture. Seventy-one percent of Cuba's exports went to the United States, and 64 percent of Cuba's imports came from the United States. Cuba exported sugar and imported candy, exported tomatoes and imported tomato paste, exported fresh fruit and imported canned fruit, exported rawhide and imported shoes, exported tobacco and imported cigarettes and cigars. It also had to import rice, beans, and potatoes to feed its population.

After World War I there was an intensive effort to develop tourism. Havana became a playground for North Americans, who arrived by plane to enjoy luxury hotels, gambling casinoes, horse racing, cabaret and nightclub shows, and beautiful mulatto prostitutes, as well as sightseeing and shopping. Vacation packages were promoted and business conventions sought. Many visitors flew in on the sixty to eighty flights a week from Miami just for an evening in the "sin capital" of the Western Hemisphere.

Tourists flocked to Cuba's beautiful beaches.

Cuba offered many pleasures of another order—spectacular beaches and golf courses, fine parks, botanical and zoological gardens, and sports centers. Havana had a museum of fine arts, an excellent symphony orchestra, and an internationally known ballet company.

Behind all this glamour and glitter (primarily in Havana), was an island full of poverty and a social pyramid much like that of the colonial era. At the top were the rich sugar magnates, importers, bankers, real estate entrepreneurs, and major merchants, who had largely replaced the old landowning families. In the next level were the lawyers, engineers, doctors, and other professionals who primarily served the rich and middle class. Further down were teachers (primary school teachers comprised half of the seventy thousand people listed as professionals by the Cuban Census of 1952) and thousands of small business people and vendors. These two levels were larger than in colonial times. At the bottom were the tenant farmers, sharecroppers, squatters, and cane cutters. Half a million cane cutters worked four months out of the year; during the remaining eight months (the dead season) they were unemployed.

U.S. POLITICAL INFLUENCE

The five decades of U.S. domination following the occupation can be divided politically into two periods—1902 to 1933 and 1934 to 1959.

First Period (1902–1933)

During the first period, the direct influence of the United States upon the political system prevented the development of centralized government.

When President Estrada secured a second term through a fraudulent election, a rebellion broke out in 1906, and he requested U.S. intervention. U.S. President Theodore Roosevelt expressed his exasperation at this turn of events in a letter to Henry White on September 13, 1906:

> Just at the moment I'm so angry with that infernal little Cuban Republic that I would like to wipe its people off the face of the earth. All that we wanted of them was that they should behave themselves and be prosperous and happy so that we would not have to interfere. And now, lo and behold, they have started an utterly unjustifiable and pointless revolution and may get things into such a snarl that we have no alternative save to intervene—which will at once convince the suspicious idiots in South America that we do wish to intervene after all.

Consequently, the United States occupied Cuba once again for more than two years, from 1906 to 1909. Estrada was forced to resign. The United States turned control over to General Charles E. Magoon, a lawyer and former governor of the Canal Zone in Panama. Magoon, however, saw his main task as one of dispensing patronage and accumulating money. When he arrived, the Cuban treasury had a balance of $13 million; when he left, it had a debt of $12 million.

U.S troops landed twice more—in 1912, to help put down racial unrest and protect United Fruit Company and Spanish-American Iron Company property, and in 1917, to help put down military confrontations protesting a fraudulent election engineered by General Mario García Menocal. The United States provided ten thousand rifles, 2 million cartridges, and five hundred marines, which enabled the reactionary Menocal to quell the protests. In gratitude, he brought Cuba into World War I and opened up the island as a training base for U.S. marines.

During this period, political parties were founded: Republicans, Conservatives, and National Liberals, all of which suffered from problems of splintering, corruption, and co-optation. In 1924 the Cuban Communist Party was founded as a reform party seeking to work through trade unions and the electoral process.

This first period ended under the harsh, repressive presidency of General Gerardo Machado Morales, who had previously been vice-president of Cuban Electric, the Havana subsidiary of a U.S. company. His term had been marked by increasing political conflict, civil unrest, worker strikes, and student protests. He imprisoned or deported thousands of political opponents, arranged the assassination of labor leaders, suppressed free speech, closed down the University of Havana, and extended his term from four to six years. In 1933, after a general strike and an Army revolt, Machado resigned and fled the country with seven bags of gold (Thomas, *Cuba or the Pursuit of Freedom*, 1998, p. 625).

Second Period (1934–1959)

The second period saw a rapid succession of presidents who represented different political perspectives, as well as financial and commercial interests. Behind them were trade unions, student groups, professional associations, and political parties across a wide spectrum from reformist to revolutionary, from advocating gradual change to fighting for radical transformation. Underneath was a strong *independista* movement that had not been stamped out by pacification, striving for the elimination of foreign control and a more equitable distribution of resources.

Older political parties continued and new ones appeared. In 1937 the Authentic Cuban Revolutionary Party (the Autenticos) claimed to be the real representatives of José Martí. In 1947 the Cuban People's Party (the Ortodoxos) claimed to represent the real revolutionary tradition. In addition, there were many smaller parties, action groups, common fronts, and grass-roots efforts dedicated to ending corruption, political oppression, police and army brutality, and economic colonialism.

In 1934 the United States and Cuba signed a new treaty abolishing the Platt Amendment but retaining the Guantánamo provisions. A new Constitution in 1940 called for universal suffrage, free elections, and political and civil liberties but did not include any mechanisms for enforcement. Political movements based on sex, class, or race were prohibited (a rule later used to put down black protests), and all political rights could be suspended for forty-five days, whenever the government judged that "security" was at risk.

Through the 1930s, a mulatto sergeant with early liberal ideas, Fulgencio Batista, began to gain influence and power, rising to the rank of colonel and then general. After a military revolt, he began, with U.S. approval, to run the government as a "strongman" behind the scenes. In 1940 he was elected president. In 1941 he brought Cuba into World War II, furnishing air and naval bases to the United States. In 1943 he legalized the Communist Party and established diplomatic relations with the Soviet Union. In 1944, after his choice of successor lost the election, he went into self-imposed exile in Florida but in 1948 was elected a Cuban senator.

In 1952, again a candidate for the presidency, Batista staged a coup d'état, suspended the Constitution, canceled elections, and became a dictator. In response, the Truman administration recognized his government and sent economic and military aid. Batista also established a close working relationship with U.S. Mafia leaders in Havana. His rule became increasingly repressive. Young people and students especially bore the brunt of the police and military violence. An estimated twenty thousand Cubans died during this time (Ruis, *Cuba for Beginners*, 1970, p. 67).

CORRUPTION IN CUBAN GOVERNMENT

These years under U.S. domination were characterized by a steady series of weak, corrupt Cuban administrations and corrupt elections as candidates competed for patronage power. The conditions for this state of affairs had been established many years before by the Spanish with their devotion to using Cuban resources for their own benefit and their political decision to situate the levers of power in Spain. It was effective preparation for Cuba's eventual incorporation into the global capitalist system.

Theses conditions were ratified and sealed by the United States when it took control of Cuba's econmy. Most Cubans, shut out of access to the national wealth, found that public administration and public works offered the greatest opportunity for financial gain. In 1903 the public payroll had expanded to 20,000 (with 8,000 in Havana). In 1911 there were 35,000 in municipal and national government jobs.

The 1898 intervention laid the basis for American control of the Cuban economy that would last until 1959. And with this control came the usual concomitant of commercial enterprise—corruption. The character of public administration in Cuba, under a U.S. client regime increasingly geared to financial opportunism, increased the likelihood of bribery and the theft of state assets. Entrepreneurs worked hard to suborn officials into offering public concessions, such as public contracts for the building of roads, bridges and government offices. One estimate suggests that through the decade of the 1910s as much as 25 per cent of customs revenue, around $8 million, was lost annually through corrupt practices, with "graft, bribery and embezzlement" serving "as the medium of political exchange." (Simons, *Cuba*, p. 221)

The breadth and depth of this problem was pointed out by Louis A. Pérez, Jr., in *Cuba: Between Reform and Revolution* (1988):

During the terms of office of José Miguel Gómez (1908–12) and Mario García Menocal (1912–20) a total of some 372 indictments were brought against public officials, dealing with a wide range of offenses, including embezzlement, fraud, homicide, infraction of postal regulations, violations of lottery law, misappropriation of funds, and violation of electoral laws. By 1923, the number of indictments had increased to 483. (p. 217)

One major source of corruption was the National Lottery, which was established in 1909 to take advantage of the popularity of gambling. It was organized into two thousand collectorships that gave each collector the privilege of selling sixteen tickets for each of the three monthly drawings. Each ticket was purchased from the lottery administration at a discounted price and sold to the public at an inflated price. Eight hundred collectorships were reserved for direct sale by the director general of the lottery, on behalf of the president. Another five hundred collectorships were distributed to senators and representatives. It was estimated that $11 million a month was raised by this means.

Another source of corruption was the Mafia. In the 1930s this U.S.-based organization with Sicilian roots, under the leadership of Meyer Lansky and Charles "Lucky" Luciano, took control of gambling in Cuba—hotel casinos and racetrack betting—developing a close working and financial relationship with President Batista. In 1956 Lanksy began building his own hotel, the Riviera, the largest casino hotel outside of Las Vegas, as his headquarters. All in all, the Mafia became responsible for a sizeable part of the Cuban economy (Simons, *Cuba*, p. 263).

Not only was the sponsorship of gambling corrupt. It also had a corrupting influence on the gambling public. Casinos, gaming tables, and the National Lottery drew the upper classes, while cockfights and street lotteries attracted the poor. Nearly every town had its cockpit. The income from these was a sort of regressive tax upon the poor—one that they could ill afford in a society characterized by poverty, unemployment, and shortage of public services.

RELIGION

In the republican period, Roman Catholicism and Afro-Cuban religions continued their ways as Evangelicalism became a larger, more influential movement.

Catholicism

The Roman Catholic Church continued to be located mainly in the cities, although, as the Catholic lawyer Raúl Gómez Treto points out in his book *The Church and Socialism in Cuba* (1988), it carried out a sporadic sacramentalizing mission in rural areas. Its Spanish character also continued. In 1955, of the 220 diocesan priests, only 95 were Cuban; of 461 priests in religious orders, only 30 were Cuban; of the 1,872 sisters, only 556 were Cuban.

The church also continued its close relationship to the upper classes and the government. In 1899 General Brooke, in an attempt to break the ties between church and state, decreed that marriages and divorces were to be civil matters from then on. Religious processions were banned, and cemeteries maintained by public funds were given to the municipalities.

In 1955 there were 212 Catholic schools, educating some 61,960 students, and three Catholic universities. Most of the students came from upper-class families. The church also operated twenty children's homes, twenty-one old people's homes, three hospitals for adults and two for children, a psychiatric sanatorium, a leper colony, an orphanage, a women's clinic, and a number of other clinics. According to Gómez Treto,

These ecclesiastical works by no means satisfied the needs of the people. Their relatively limited scope and the fact that they were concentrated in cities, and indeed in well-off neighborhoods—the only way they could make ends meet and perhaps turn a profit—meant that most people did not benefit from them. This situation was not a scandal in a dependent, consumption-minded, underdeveloped capitalist society where the overriding principle was that of profit. On the contrary, the limited extent of these works carried out by the church for the poor of the nation was in itself a prophetic sign of what a society more just than the existing one would be, but the sign was insufficient and scarcely noticeable. (pp. 13–14)

Evangelical Churches

In 1899 U.S. General Brook also granted freedom for Protestant missions to work in Cuba, and U.S. mission boards (Presbyterian, Methodist, Baptist, Episcopalian, and others) began sending missionaries to establish churches and schools. The Methodist church in Matanzas, built in 1900, was the first Protestant church building erected in Cuba. Methodists soon established churches in all the provinces.

Beginning in 1899 both the Northern and Southern Presbyterians sent missionaries. Rev. Pedro Rioseco, a Sunday school missionary from Philadelphia, arrived in Havana to start worship services, a Sunday school, and a parish day school for children. In 1901 Rev. Joseph Milton Greene (former president of Presbyterian Seminary in Mexico City) arrived to organize officially the Northern Presbyterian pastoral work in Havana. In 1904 the Presbytery of Cuba was formed, and the cornerstone of the First Presbyterian Church in Havana, pastored by Greene, was laid in 1906. In 1899 Rev. John G. Hall was sent by the Southern Presbyterians to establish a

This baroque-style Second Baptist Church in Santiago de Cuba was built in the 1940s.

center of operations in Cárdenas: a church, an orphanage, and the first Westminster Fellowship.

In 1899 the Home Missionary Society of the Congregational Churches sent missionaries to organize churches, Sunday schools, and day schools. In 1909 this work was transferred to the Northern Presbyterian Church. In 1910 three other early pastors also transferred to the Presbyterian Church—Rev. Enrique B. Someillan, founder of the Methodist Church in Cuba (because of disagreements with the hierarchy), Dr. Albert J. Diaz, founder of the Baptist work in Cuba in 1883 (because of clashes with the Southern Baptist Church), and Rev. Pedro Duarte, founder of the Episcopal church (because of administrative controversies).

In 1899 the Disciples of Christ sent L. C. McPherson and Melvin Menges, who first preached to the U.S. forces. They opened a school in Havana and a church and school in Matanzas. In 1917 this work was transferred to the Presbyterian Church.

The Southern Baptists began work in the western half of the island, and the Northern Baptists in the eastern end; the Friends started in the eastern end, and the Episcopalians began in all six provinces. The Church of God, Salvation Army, and West Indies Mission also started work in Cuba.

The members in these Evangelical churches, in contrast to those in the Catholic churches, generally came from the poorer working classes. A questionnaire in the late 1930s revealed that 51 percent of the members of the average Cuban church were in debt, chiefly as a result of the long dead season of the sugar industry, illness, low wages, bad harvest, the economic depression, unemployment, and the rise in the cost of living. This situation raised a crucial question for the early U.S. mission effort: How could a relatively expensive institution, a product of an alien, high-grade economy and living standards, be indigenized and financed in countries of lower economic standards where the bulk of the church members were drawn from the classes of the lowest economic levels?

Another mission problem soon arose: The founders of Cuban churches brought with them the conservative social point of view and strict discipline of the U.S. churches from an earlier period. They built that discipline into the Cuban churches and rigidly held to it, training Cuban pastors to it in spite of a more liberal belief and practice that by that time had arisen in many U.S. churches. Churches that forbade drinking, dancing, and gambling had a difficult time gaining members in a society long accustomed to such pleasures.

Beyond the evangelistic effort of starting new congregations, mission work in Cuba branched out in many other directions. In 1917 an

Evangelical bookstore, La Nueva Senda (The New Path), was opened under the auspices of the Presbyterians in Havana.

Many Evangelical churches founded schools. The Methodists operated Candler College (a high school), Buenavista School for Girls, and the Central Methodist School, all in Havana. They also built a university church and dormitory for students two blocks from the University of Havana. In Oriente Province, the Agricultural and Industrial School of Preston was started in 1944 on land donated by the United Fruit Company, with support from the Methodists, United Fruit employees, and friends. La Progresiva School of the Presbyterians in Cárdenas, starting with fourteen students in 1900, eventually turned into a twelve-grade school for two thousand boarding and day students. The Presbyterians also maintained numerous other grade schools and church schools. The Baptists founded El Cristo School in Oriente Province, and the Friends established the Friends College in Holguín. (Batista was a graduate of this school.) In 1955 there were some fifty Evangelical schools.

The Methodists and Presbyterians founded the Evangelical Theological Seminary at Matanzas in 1946; the Episcopalians joined them a year later. Evangelical churches also operated dispensaries and clinics.

One of the early Presbyterian missionaries, Janet Houston, expressed in a letter some of her feelings about the church's mission in the midst of the overwhelming U.S. presence:

The Americans come to Cuba to raise cattle and to sow tomatoes and green peppers, to build highways and sell merchandise, to make the ports deeper and clean the streets, to kill the mosquitoes and vaccinate the children, to train militarily and to construct warships, to look for oil and gold, to play baseball and to race cars on Sundays, to buy thousands of acres of this black land, and to place merchant ships in these blue waters, until the Cubans say that this island will come to belong completely to the Americans. And in the midst of all this, our church, and all the other evangelical churches have here a small flock of torch bearers that are like small fireflies in the darkness of the vast night. (Rafael Cepeda, *Apuntes para una Hisoria del Presbiterianisme en Cuba*, 1986, p. 52)

Rafael Cepeda, in his book *Notes for a History of Presbyterianism in Cuba*, describes some of the positive and negative characteristics of the Protestant missionary work in this early period. One of the great positives was the good ecumenical relations maintained by the early missionaries. In 1902 the First Conference of Evangelical Pastors in Cuba was held in Cienfuegos with Baptists, Congregationalist, Disciples, Methodists, Friends, and Presbyterians gathered together. In 1905 the Nation Association of Sunday Schools was organized, and in 1906 the first Youth Convention was held in Matanzas.

In 1905 the Young Men's Christian Association (YMCA) was founded in Cuba. In 1920 a Christian Workers' Club was opened. (In response, the Catholic bishop in Havana condemned the YMCA and threatened to excommunicate those who participated in its activities.) The next year Methodist, Presbyterian, Episcopal, and Baptist pastors attended a YMCA meeting to discuss measures to deter the immorality rampant in the city.

On the negative side of the ledger, according to Cepeda, Evangelical missionaries in Cuba made several basic errors: 1. Moralism: They believed that the immediate problems in Cuba could be solved by not drinking alcoholic beverages, not smoking, not dancing, keeping the Sabbath, not attending cockfights, and avoiding other popular customs. 2. Idealism: They affirmed that a good republic could be built just by establishing Protestant schools and churches. 3. Conformism: They accepted without analysis or reflection the concepts of an expansionist era portrayed by U.S. newspapers, often loaded with "patriotic," " humanitarian," and "religious" falsehoods (pp. 56–57).

Moreover, many missionaries, reflecting U.S. perspectives, denied blacks entrance to mission schools. Most blacks could not afford even modest fees and lived far from cities, where most schools were, but racial prejudice was also involved. U.S. Protestants had brought with them the wine of the gospel in the wineskins of a North American mentality characterized by an individualistic ethic and the sense that Cubans were theologically, intellectually, and economically dependent.

A typical response of the Evangelical Cuban churches to the problem of hunger and poverty in those years was the collection of food and clothing to be distributed among the poor on Nochebuena (December 24). For example, in one Cuban city in 1924 a paper bag containing rice, corn meal, sugar, coffee, plantain, guava paste, cheese, bread, meat, soap, and a Scripture tract from the American Bible Society was given to each poor person. In Cuba today, where poverty has been addressed systemically by the communist government, such gifts are no longer the custom, although they still continue in the United States.

J. Merle Davis, of the International Missionary Council, made a study of the economic and social basis of the Evangelical churches in Cuba. In *The Cuban Church in a Sugar Economy* (1942), he asked several important questions: "How can a small and obscure society lift itself out of the dilemma which engulfs the whole community of which it is a part?" and "At what point or in what manner can the Church, or any agency of human betterment, take hold of such a situation with hope of a permanent remedy?" (p. 90). Perhaps answers for these questions were given to the Cuban church by the revolutionary events of 1959. Davis also made an important observation: "The Cuban Church of the future may be expected to differ from the American Church in its structure and emphasis. The gospel of Christ will make itself most fully felt in Cuba when it appeals to the sources of Cuban ideology and motivation, and when its roots find that nourishment in Cuba rather than in the United States" (p. 8).

In December 1942, the Methodist evangelist E. Stanley Jones conducted a twelve-day preaching mission in Cuba. In his final message to the Cuban people, given at a Baptist church in Havana, he presented a thirteen–point Reconstruction Plan given below. Most of it, interestingly, was later put into operation by Cuba's new revolutionary government.

1. An order based on equality of opportunity for all, without race, creed, class, or sex distinctions.
2. Honest officials, elected in honest elections, administering their posts honestly, and supported by civic conscience.
3. Decentralization of authority, each municipality feeling directly responsible for civic improvements.
4. Popular movements for public improvements such as paving of streets, drainage of cities, pure and abundant water, elimination of slums, improvement of general sanitary conditions, adequate hospitals.
5. Rural reconstruction; a movement back to the country, with adequate reconstruction of rural life.
6. Regulation for the sugar industry in the interests of the people.
7. Creation of new trades and industries to give employment to the workers during the "dead season", also cultivation of reserved and unused land.
8. A minimum wage scale for working classes, including domestic servants.
9. Elimination of illiteracy (calculated at 35%) within ten years, through adult education.
10. An adequate diet for the people.
11. Elimination of the lottery and all other forms of gambling.
12. Purification and strengthening of home life—making common law marriages a shameful custom.
13. A faith for the people that purifies morally, awakens intellectually, and produces hope for the future. (Mitchel, *Cuba Calling*, 1949, pp. 66–67)

THE THIRD WAR FOR INDEPENDENCE:
THE TRIUMPH OF THE REVOLUTION

When the third phase of Cuba's hundred-year struggle for independence began, it was the eastern province of Oriente that once again proved to be the "Cradle of the Revolution." But this time the struggle was led by youth and especially by two men who came from very different backgrounds: Fidel Castro and Frank País.

Fidel Castro, (see box) the lawyer son of a well-to-do sugar planter, became convinced that revolution was the only way to oust Batista and free Cuba from corruption and U.S. domination. He and a group of rebels decided to start the revolution by attacking the Moncada barracks in Santiago. One night 150 young men—mostly lower-middle class or workers and a few students—met on a farm east of Santiago.

In the early hours of July 26, 1953, they attacked the barracks. Fifty got lost in the dark streets, and an auto accident at the barracks cost them the element of surprise. Most of the rest were caught, tortured, and killed. The thirty survivors fled into the mountains, were captured, and through the efforts of a sympathetic black officer, were handed over to the municipal jail rather than to Batista's soldiers. At their trial in Santiago October 16, they were condemned to fifteen years in prison.

A Rebel Patriot Who Succeeded

Fidel Castro was born August 13, 1926, near Biran, in Oriente Province, where his father had a large sugar plantation. The area was dominated by four large U.S. companies. He and his brothers, Ramón and Raúl, were sent to Catholic primary schools in Santiago. Fidel went on to Belen, a secondary school run by Jesuits in Havana. From 1945 to 1950 he studied law at the University of Havana, where he took an active role in political discussion and agitation through various students' groups advocating socialism and revolution. He spoke out increasingly against the "betrayed revolution" of 1898, corruption in government, and foreign ownership of most of Cuba's wealth. He graduated with several law degrees.

Fidel (as he is known and addressed by everyone in Cuba) decided to run for a seat in Congress, but the election was aborted by Batista's coup in 1952. Fidel then began to organize political action cells but soon decided that the needed action was "revolutionary, not political: To a revolutionary party there must correspond a young and revolutionary leadership, of popular origin, which will save Cuba."

With fellow rebels in Havana he planned to open a third war for independence by attacking the Moncada barracks in Santiago at the trial. The attack failed, and in Santiago, Fidel defended himself in a passionate speech, ending "History will absolve me." He was sent to prison where he taught himself Cuban history, while his speech was circulated by his supporters around Cuba.

Released from prison by an amnesty in 1955, Fidel started to organize the 26 July Movement to carry on the struggle. Distrusting the amnesty, he and his fellow rebels fled to Mexico. They returned on the yacht *Granma* in December 1956, but most were killed by Batista's soldiers. Fidel and eleven others headed into the mountains, where they lived with the peasants and gradually gathered recruits and arms. After two years of guerrilla warfare, they succeeded in toppling Batista. Fidel Castro became head of a new revolutionary government and turned to the task of solving Cuba's problems by Cuban means.

Castro's speech at the trial, however, was widely circulated by other concerned Cuban activists, including Frank País (see box). Indeed, the speech became a defining moment of the revolution, expressing a passion for justice as the social and economic situation worsened.

Released by a decree of amnesty after just two years, the rebels began to organize the 26 July Movement but soon left for Mexico to escape harassment by Batista soldiers. There they were joined by Ernesto ("Che") Guevera, an Argentinian doctor, who quickly became one of Castro's right-hand men.

A Rebel Patriot Who Was Shot

Frank País was born December 7, 1934, in the small parsonage of the First Baptist Church in Santiago, where his father was minister. When Frank was five, his father died. Frank took on the responsibility of helping his mother raise two younger brothers, Josué and Agustín. He went to primary school and one year of secondary school at the Martí Institute run by the Baptist church and then entered normal school to become a teacher. Mature for his age, he was a leader in student associations.

Outraged by corruption in government and the " betrayed revolution" of José Martí, he was also disillusioned by the failure of political leaders to fight Batista after the 1952 coup. He led protests and demonstrations in Santiago, organized the normal school students, and joined national parties for revolution and liberation. After graduating in 1953, he taught at El Salvador secondary school run by the Second Baptist Church. Educated in music by his mother, he also became organist and choir director at the church. At the same time he was studying education at the University of Santiago and teaching as a volunteer at a school for workers in the university. As he became more familiar with the miserable life of most peasants, his passion to help poor Cubans increased. He began to organize students and workers in a movement that included propaganda, finance, and action.

Frank País, right, churchman and teacher, played a leading role in the revolution of 1959.

Castro's attack on the Moncada barracks surprised Frank, who ran there to discover the bloody scene. Later, when he read Fidel's speech at the trial, it became for him a moment of "historical transcendence," for it expressed his own deepest thoughts. Recognizing the speech as a program and vision for the nation, he had it printed and distributed it widely.

When Fidel was released from prison, Frank (as he was known in Cuba) placed himself under Fidel's command. He became chief of action in Oriente, organizing action cells, sabotage, and weapons for what he considered the necessary war against Batista. He also began leading assaults on police stations to capture arms. In August 1956 he and other leaders of the 26 July Movement went to Mexico to coordinate plans with Castro. Fidel, tremendously impressed by the young revolutionary, wrote to the treasurer of the movement in Oriente: "Everything you told me about the magnificent conditions of organization, and the bravery and capacity of Frank, is true." He then made Frank national chief of action.

On returning to Santiago, Frank resigned his job at El Salvador, telling the pastors, "You'll need to find somebody else for my place, because Cuba needs me." He then began to prepare for uprisings and other actions to coincide with Fidel's return. When Fidel and the other survivors fled to the mountains, Frank supplied them with equipment, guns, and fifty-three new recruits.

In the summer of 1957, the Batista forces intensified their search for Frank. He started using a disguise and moving from house to house in Santiago for protection. Finally, on July 30, one of his former students recognized him and identified him to the police, who gunned him down on the street. The whole city turned out for Frank País's funeral—a silent procession, the largest demonstration that had ever taken place in Santiago. Expressions of praise and sorrow from Fidel, Che Guevara, and other leaders for this twenty-three-year-old mentioned his maturity, humility, discipline, intelligence, and integrity. He remained a devout Christian and devout revolutionary all through his life. As one person put it, his hands were equally at home at the organ keyboard or holding a gun on behalf of Cuban independence.

~~~~~~~~~~~~~~~~~~~~~~~~~~~~~~~~~~

Meanwhile the 26 July Movement continued in Cuba, led by País and others. One of its projects was to raise money to buy the yacht *Granma* to bring the rebels back from Mexico. An important participant in this effort was Rev. Rafael Cepeda, a Presbyterian pastor and treasurer of the 26 July Movement in Matzanzas Province.

The *Granma* left Mexico with eighty-two men on November 27, 1956. Overloaded and delayed by storms, it did not arrive till December 2. By that time a rising in Santiago on November 30, planned by País to coincide with Castro's landing, had been crushed. No longer a surprise, the rebels were nearly all destroyed by Batista's waiting soldiers. The remnants took refuge in the Sierra Maestra. There in the mountains they launched guerrilla attacks on the much hated Rural Guards and came to understand more fully the great economic and social needs of the poor who sheltered them. Recruits and arms slowly flowed in, some brought by País.

There were also armed student uprisings in the cities, even before Castro's return. In Havana March 13, 1957, a group of university students, led by a Catholic student, José Antonio Echevarría, made an assault on the presidential palace in an attempt to assassinate Batista. They failed, and thirty-two of the thirty-five students, including Echevarría, were killed. In Matanzas in November the government caught a member of the 26 July Movement who, under torture, revealed the name of Rafael Cepeda as one of the leaders of the movement. Police went to his house to arrest him, but he was at a Rotary meeting, where a fellow pastor warned him and helped him escape by plane to Miami. (He returned to Cuba in 1959.)

Batista sent forces into Oriente Province, where columns of revolutionaries led by Fidel and Raúl Castro, Che Guevara, and Camilo Cienfuegos were stepping up operations. Rebel forces gradually expanded west, destroying plantation crops and other property wherever possible, creating shortages of food and oil, so that the upper and middle classes would lose confidence in Batista. Confidence was further shaken by an army revolt against Batista and news that in March the U.S. government, which had hitherto maintained close ties with Batista, stopped sending him arms. More and more government troops defected or joined the revolutionaries. In late December an armored train with reinforcements sent by Batista to Oriente was derailed, and Santa Clara and Santiago fell to the rebels. On January 1, 1959, Batista fled to the Dominican Republic. His press secretary estimated his fortune in 1958 to be about $300 million, invested abroad (Thomas, *Cuba or the Pursuit of Freedom*, p. 1027). On January 8, Castro and his men entered a jubilant Havana.

Questions for Reflection

1. Compare the attitude of U.S. Protestant missionaries toward Cubans with the attitude of the Spanish Catholic missionaries and clergy. What similarities and differences were there in their behavior?
2. How would a Cuban landowner feel as U.S. businessmen bought up Cuban land and industry? How would a landless worker feel? Would he be better off under a Cuban or a U.S. employer?
3. What was the attitude of the United States, "land of the free," toward Cuban independence? Why?
4. Given the obstacles in the way of Cuba's struggle for independence, what are some of the reasons for its success?

Chapter 3

Cuba Under Cuban Management

Many people, overjoyed to have won true independence at last, welcomed Castro with signs that said *"Gracias Fidel."* But as Fidel reminded the people in Havana, the struggle was not over. Although the revolution had triumphed, it was to be a continuing process of development and transformation.

A Period of Transition (1959–1961)

At the top of the agenda was gaining control over the economy. Although U.S. political control of Cuba through pliant Cuban presidents and treaties had been broken, the United States still controlled Cuba's economy. How to bring about a transformation in this area after 450 years was a daunting challenge for young revolutionaries in their twenties and thirties. They had no experience in running a government—only Martí's dreams of an independent republic built "with all and for the good of all," committed to justice, an equitable distribution of wealth, and freedom from racial discrimination.

To get the process under way, they set up a provisional government, made up of middle-class moderates who had participated in previous administrations and independence organizations. These men had all opposed Batista, but their ideas of moderate reform did not mesh well with the more radical perspectives of the peasant, worker, and student rebels who wanted a thorough reordering of society. As a result, the government leadership underwent a number of changes.

Early Reforms

In its early months the new government, with Castro as prime minister, took a number of reformist actions to help ameliorate the plight of the rural and urban poor. It cut in half the electric power rates for rural areas, reduced urban housing rents by 30 to 50 percent, lowered mortgage and telephone rates, opened up private beaches to the public on an integrated basis, and seized the gambling casinos run by the Mafia. But it soon became clear that the economy needed much more than piecemeal reform. Edward Boorstein refers to this "much more" in a series of provocative questions in his book *The Economic Transformation of Cuba* (1968): How far could Cuba go to cure its economy without antagonizing American imperialism? Would higher wages for sugar workers solve the problem of the dead period? Could a true land reform, which means taking land away from large estates and giving it to all the people, be accomplished without hurting some of them? A true land reform changes the balance of political power; it is not a *reform*; it is a *revolutionary* measure. Could the large foreign corporations in Cuba be reformed in ways that touched the heart of Cuba's problems? In short, could a Cuban government do anything to solve Cuba's problems without disrupting some American interest? If it tried, what could be expected from the United States? As Boorstein summed it up,

No matter where you start probing the Cuban economy, if you cut at all deep you will hit the core of the malignancy—American imperialism. Cuba had many problems. But its chief problem was the United States. The precondition for being able to make a serious attack on Cuba's specific problems was the elimination of imperialism. A true revolution in Cuba had to be a revolution against American imperialism. (p.16)

The rural poor benefited from electrification, enabling them to enjoy television.

Land Reform and Nationalization

From this point on, the Cuban government became more radical. On May 17, 1959, it passed the first Agrarian Reform law, limiting the amount of land one person could hold, expropriating the rest, and distributing it to 25,000 farm families. This expropriation process, which affected especially the great landowners, expanded rapidly. A second Agrarian Reform law, in 1963, eliminated landowners of middle-size and large properties. Eventually the state owned 70 percent of all land, which was not redistributed.

Many people do not know that the right to expropriate land for the national interest was already in Cuba's 1940 Constitution and had been affirmed by the UN in 1952. Nor do they know that Cuba proposed compensation with government-issued bonds that paid an annual interest of 4.5 percent and were to be refunded in twenty years. (This was actually more generous than the bonds issued by General Douglas MacArthur in occupied Japan, which limited interest to 2.5 percent and refunding to twenty-four years.)

All the other foreign countries with investments in Cuba—France, Switzerland, Great Britain, Canada, and Spain—accepted Cuba's plan, but the United States objected. It asked Cuba for "the payment of a prompt, adequate, and effective compensation." In 1964 the U.S. Supreme Court supported the international legality of Cuba's expropriation actions, but this decision was overruled by Congress. The Hickenlooper Amendment to the 1964 Foreign Assistance Act called Cuban nationalizations contrary to international law because they offered "no compensation," the same argument used by Congress today! (Incidentally, the United States does not have a very good record on compensation. Out of its 4 million inhabitants in 1776, approximately a hundred thousand dissenters—those loyal to King George III—were expatriated to England, and all their properties were confiscated without compensation.)

In 1960 conflict between Cuba and the United States intensified. In January the Cuban government expropriated 70,000 acres of property owned by U.S. sugar companies, including 35,000 acres of pastures and forest land in Oriente Province belonging to the United Fruit Company. This action immediately placed Cuba in direct opposition to high U.S. government officials. Secretary of State John Foster Dulles had been a stockholder and legal adviser for United Fruit; his brother, Allen W. Dulles, director of the Central Intelligence Agency (CIA), had been a director and a former president of the corporation. UN Ambassador Henry Cabot Lodge had also been a director; and Walter Bedell Smith, former CIA director, had also been a president of the corporation.

Opposition solidified in July, when Cuba nationalized all U.S.–owned properties in Cuba, offering its standard twenty-year compensation. These properties included thirty-six sugar mills and lands, all U.S. refineries and other oil properties, and all electric power and telephone companies. Expanding its policy, on October 13 Cuba nationalized all companies (foreign and Cuban) dealing with sugar, distilled spirits, beverages, soap, perfume, milk products, packing devices, chemicals, maritime transportation, construction work, railway communications, retail products, coffee, drugs and pharmaceutical products, and the banking system. Hotels were also nationalized, which meant that the Mafia lost its huge profit from hotels, gambling, and prostitution in Cuba. On October 14, Cuba transferred all housing to tenants and paid compensation to landlords.

One of the defining moments in this transition period came on April 16, 1961, at the funeral service for victims of bomb attacks by Cuban exiles (see below) when Castro declared the socialist nature of the revolution. He repeated this declaration at his May Day speech several weeks later. From now on, socialism was to be the official context for Cuba's nationalization and development process. In some ways, it was a logical next step, for the government believed that nationalization of the large sugar plantations required state-sponsored development and central planning. Nevertheless, the announcement came as a shock for the upper class, for Cubans with a North American mentality, and especially for those church members who believed that anything to do with socialism or communism was anathema. The trauma of this event was one of the chief reasons many such Cubans migrated to the United States (as discussed in chapter 4).

It is especially interesting to note why the masses turned in favor of socialism. Juan Antonio Blanco in his conversation with Medea Benjamin, in the book *Cuba: Talking About Revolution* (1997), gives a clue:

When the United States began fomenting overt and covert hostility toward Cuba—as early as May 1959—it unwittingly also began a process of educating the Cuban masses in the socialist alternative. The Cuban people began to see socialism as the only alternative to the kind of society in which they had previously lived and to the kind of relationship they had formerly had with the United States. And they began to see that the only way to resist the aggression of the United States was to radicalize the revolution in order to defeat the United States and its local allies. This included befriending the Soviet Union and Eastern Europe in order to create a relationship of forces that could preserve Cuba's sovereignty. (p.15)

U.S. HOSTILITY

In this and subsequent sections, many actions are ascribed to the United States that may be startling to some readers. They are supported by the sources listed parenthetically or in the bibliography.

Even before Castro's victory, the United States was beginning to view Cuba as a developing "malignancy" in its own backyard—a threat, by its independent actions, to U.S. authority and Cuba's "manifest destiny" as the United States perceived it. The United States started a counterrevolutionary campaign almost immediately after Castro's entry into Havana. In January 1959 the CIA began hiring former soldiers of Batista's army in Florida to take part in an invasion of Cuba from the Dominican Republic. It was to be coordinated with plans for an internal insurrection and destabilization, thus setting the scene for military intervention from the United States. The plot, however, was uncovered by Cuba and foiled.

In March, the U.S. National Security Council met in secret session to discuss how to install a new government in Cuba. After this, attempts on Castro's life and sabotage against sugar mills, cane fields, and public buildings increased significantly. According to General Fabian Escalante, former head of Cuban State Security, from 1959 to 1993 there were 612 documented assassination plots against Castro (*CIA Targets Fidel*, 1996, p.8).

In April 1959 Castro was invited by the American Society of Newspaper Editors to give several talks in the United States. He received a warm reception in New York and Boston, but President Dwight Eisenhower refused to meet with him, substituting a hostile Vice President Richard Nixon. The next month Nixon and executives of Pepsi Cola, Esso, Standard Oil, United Fruit, and the Mafia met secretly, offering support for Nixon's candidacy in exchange for his promise to overthrow the Cuban government (Simons, *Cuba*, p. 292).

Cuba's policy of nationalization was countered by increasingly hostile actions by the United States: In January 1960 the CIA, with the approval of the National Security Council, began Operation 40 to come up with "alternative solutions to the Cuban problem." These solutions included psychological warfare, diplomatic and economic pressures, and clandestine activity. The physical elimination of Fidel Castro was one of the top priorities (Escalante, *Secret War*, 1995, pp.41–42; Funati, *ZR Rifle*, 1994, pp. 14–16; Hinckle and Turner, *Deadly Secrets*, 1993, pp. 365–67). On the economic front, the United States stopped importing Cuban sugar, causing Cuba to sell sugar to China and the Soviet bloc in exchange for food, machinery, and crude oil. Later, the United States declared an embargo on U.S. trade with Cuba.

In March, a Belgian ship bringing arms and ammunition for the Cuban government was blown up, resulting in the death of a hundred Cuban workers and soldiers and the wounding of two hundred. The CIA began training mercenary recruits in Florida and Guatemala and distributing various kinds of poisons to the Mafia to use on Castro (Simons, *Cuba*, pp. 304–07; *CIA Targets Castro*, pp. 34–37).

At the end of 1960 the CIA inaugurated, with the cooperation of State Department officials and the head of the Catholic Service Bureau of Florida, a psychological warfare program called Operation Peter Pan. It was then carried out through one of the CIA-related counterrevolutionary organizations in Cuba, the People's Revolutionary Movement.

Copies of a fake *Patria Potestad* law, supposedly issued by the Cuban government for the purpose of taking children away from their parents and sending them to the Soviet Union for education, were circulated. In the resulting hysteria and panic, fifteen thousand children were sent away by their families to camps and foster homes in Florida between December 1960 and October 1962. Most were joined by their parents in the next several years (Furiati, *ZR Rifle*, p. 37).

Also at the end of 1960 the CIA revived and revised, under the name of Operation Pluto, its 1959 plot for an invasion from the Domincan Republic. It eventually resulted in the Bay of Pigs invasion in 1961. On April 15, planes flown by Cuban exiles bombed Cuban airfields. The Cuban government promptly imprisoned thousands of Cubans it suspected of hostility to the government. On April 17, the 1,500-man, CIA-organized invasion force led by Manuel Artime, a former leader of the Jesuit-founded University Catholic Group, landed at Playa Giron. Each mercenary wore the emblem of Brigade 2506—the Cuban flag and the Christian cross. The brigade was named after the serial number of a member, a Catholic student, who was killed accidentally while training. One of the three Spanish priests accompanying the group stated their position: "The assault brigade is made of thousands of Cubans who are all Christians and Catholics. Our struggle is that of those who believe in God against the atheists, the struggle of democracy against communism."

The invaders, not receiving support from the Cuban population or from the U.S. government, were defeated within seventy-two hours. Some thousand were taken prisoner. Among them were men who previously owned in Cuba 914,859 acres of land, 9,666 houses, 70 factories, 5 mines, 2 banks, and 10 sugar mills. (Thomas, *Cuba or the Pursuit of Freedom*, p. 1361). They were eventually released upon payment by the United States of $53 million in food and medicine.

Castro's declaration of Cuba's socialism confirmed the worst fears of the United States and gave new urgency to its efforts to destroy the Cuban revolution. In May 1961 the CIA initiated Operation Patty to assassinate the Castro brothers. In November the U.S. government organized Operation Mongoose, integrating the resources of the CIA, Pentagon, State Department, and U.S. Information Agency in an effort to "solve" the Cuban problem. Strategies were developed for both inside and outside

Cuba to undermine, destabilize, and overthrow the Cuban government and to demoralize the Cuban people and encourage them to revolt. Incorporated into Operation Mongoose was ZR-Rifle, a CIA program to assassinate foreign leaders such as Patrice Lumumba, R. L. Trujillo, and Castro (Furiati, *ZR Rifle*, pp. 40–44, 128–30).

In February 1962 President John F. Kennedy declared a commercial blockade of Cuba, which prohibited other countries from exporting to Cuba products that contained U.S. technology. In addition, Congress prohibited any U.S. economic aid to governments that supported Cuba.

As the Colombian novelist Gabriel García Márquez wrote,

> That night, the first of the blockade, there were in Cuba some 482,550 cars, 343,300 refrigerators, 549,700 radios, 303,500 TV sets, 352,900 electric irons, 288,400 fans, 41,800 washing machines, 3,510,000 wrist watches, 63 locomotives, and 12 merchant ships. All these, except the watches which were Swiss, were made in the United States. . . . From the point of view of production, Cuba found that it was not a country in its own right, but a commercial peninsula of the USA. (*Cuba Update*, April 1990)

ORGANIZING AN ALTERNATIVE SOCIETY (1961–1991)

Meanwhile the revolutionary government was trying to fashion a new society that would not repeat the injustices of the old. Limited in resources and experience, it found its earliest successes in social development rather than in the areas of economics and politics.

Social Development

Cuba made remarkable strides in the areas of education, health, and the position of women and blacks.

Education for All. Although Cuba had a higher rate of literacy than the rest of Latin America, about a quarter of the population could not read. Education was declared a human right and made available to everyone free of charge. For the first time in Cuban history, whites, blacks, mulattos, girls, and boys, of all classes, had equal opportunity to go to school and to go through all levels from primary, to secondary, to university or technical school. But the first challenge was to teach everyone to read.

On January 1, 1961, the National Literacy Campaign was begun—a program that in a single year reduced the rate of illiteracy from 25 percent to 3.9 percent. Schools were closed, and 95,000 students between the ages of nine and nineteen (more than half of them girls and women) were recruited, trained for a week, equipped with two basic reading books and a paraffin lamp (plus a uniform, blanket, and hammock), and sent out to teach a million illiterates how to read.

Beyond increasing literacy, the program had a profound effect upon the whole nation. It gave participants a sense of being engaged in a mutual teaching-learning experience and one that was important to the building of a nation. One of the slogans of the campaign was "You will learn more than you teach." The volunteers who lived among the poor peasants for those months returned to the cities with deeper understanding of why the poor areas of the nation needed to be given preferential treatment by the revolution. Counterrevolutionaries, disapproving of this effort, assassinated four volunteer teachers (Franklin, *Cuba and the United States*, 1997, pp. 34, 37, 44, 45).

After the literacy campaign, the first educational goal was a sixth-grade level for everyone, then a ninth-grade level. The government started primary schools in former military barracks and in some of the large houses abandoned by rich Cubans who fled. It established secondary schools, technical schools, and universities all over the country within reach of the citizens of each province. It started night schools to help adults catch up, although there was often a lack of trained teachers.

In pre-revolutionary Cuba, as in most of Latin America, education had been chiefly in the liberal arts. Secondary schools prepared students for universities, where they gained degrees in the humanities or law, making an overabundance of graduates in those fields. After 1959 the focus shift-

All Cuban children, girls and boys, black and white, can attend state schools free of charge.

ed to technical and scientific training, especially needed to replace the middle-class professionals who had left the country. The shift was most marked at university level, where career choices were often restricted to fields, such as agriculture, where national needs were greatest.

The new focus was also reflected in the secondary boarding schools built in the countryside. These schools, organized on a study-work basis, and housing 250 boys and 250 girls for five days a week, were placed in the midst of agriculture areas and were designed to give students an opportunity to take part in the development of the nation, as well as to keep intellectual endeavor close to manual work on the land, as José Martí had urged. Each morning half the students would take class work while the other half worked in the fields or orchards. In the afternoon, the two groups would switch. The schools were staffed by professionals and directed by a student council and a parents' advisory council.

Specialized schools were started for students with seeing, hearing, or motor problems—where medical attention and therapy could be offered along with academic classes. On the Isle of Youth secondary boarding schools were opened for thousands of students from Africa, Nicaragua, Korea, and Yemen. The schools use teachers from the students' home country and from Cuba. Graduates can return home or attend a Cuban university. At one point there were sixty such schools, but the program had to be curtailed in the 1990s because of expense.

Health Care for All. Health care was declared a human right and made available to everyone free of charge. Between 1958 and 1975 Cuba's public budget increased by twenty times, and by 1996, 21.5 percent of it was devoted to health care and education. The infant mortality rate was reduced from 60 per 1,000 live births in the 1950s to 9.4 in 1995, among the lowest in the world. Life expectancy increased from fifty-five years to seventy-six. In 1995 the United Nations Children's Fund (UNICEF) honored Cuba for its positive achievements as a developing society.

The number of hospitals increased from 58 in 1959 (mostly private or religious with 60 percent of beds in Havana) to 256 in 1989 (government owned, with 60 percent of beds in rural areas). There are now many hospitals specializing in pediatrics, maternity care, cancer, cardiology, ophthalmology, and psychiatry. The top hospital, Hermanos Ameijeiras in Havana, offers high-technology medicine both to Cubans and needy patients from other parts of Latin America, all free of charge.

In addition to hospitals, since 1965 the government has established polyclinics around the country. These neighborhood health centers, staffed by medical personnel plus a social worker, are open twenty-four hours a day.

Cuba has also spent huge amounts of money on biotechnology and pharmaceutical research. Cuban scientists have produced cholesterol-reducing PPG, interferon for cancer treatment, a vaccine against hepatitis B and meningitis B, an epidermal growth factor for healing, streptokinase for heart attacks, and other pioneering drugs.

In 1984 Castro himself conceived a new health-care approach, the Family Doctor Program. It was introduced first in the Sierra Maestra and then all over the country. The program places a family doctor in the midst of, and responsible for, 125 families. A specially designed building has a waiting room, doctor's office, and examination/treatment room on the first floor and the doctor's living quarters on the second. Office hours are in the morning; afternoons are usually spent in home visits and at the local hospital. The doctors are on call, however, twenty-four hours a day. By living close to their assigned families for two-year terms, the family doctors become familiar with the psycho-socio-biological problems of their patients. They give special attention to senior citizens and often serve, too, as counselors to families and young people. There is a strong emphasize on holistic health care.

According to Julie M. Feinsilver in *Healing the Masses: Cuban Health Politics at Home and Abroad* (1993),

> The fundamental task of the family doctor is to aggressively investigate and monitor the health of the entire population, not just the diseased. This is an extraordinary effort to assess the health of all people, promote their physical fit-

Since the revolution, doctors, paid by the state, are assigned to serve units of 125 local families. Many doctors are women.

ness, detect risk factors for disease, prevent and cure disease, and provide rehabilitation services. (Berkeley: University of California Press, p. 40)

Cuba also has a number of rural health centers in resortlike settings with a swimming pool, offering programs focusing on stress, obesity, hypertension, asthma, and problems of the elderly. The program includes medical evaluations, psychoanalysis, and energometric assessment and offers educational opportunities, therapeutic exercises, relaxation techniques, hypnosis, acupuncture, massage, and indoor and outdoor sports.

Robert N. Ubell writes,

> Cuban medical school graduates no longer take the Hippocratic oath. Instead, they promise to abide by new revolutionary principles: renunciation of private practice and agreement to serve in rural areas, to practice in the name of the people, to promote preventive medicine and human welfare, to strive for scientific excellence and political devotion, to encourage proletarian internationalism, and to defend the Cuban Revolution. ("Twenty-five Years of Cuban Health Care," in Brenner, *The Cuba Reader*, 1989, p.441)

Medical salaries are the same all over Cuba, depending upon years of service and specialization; therefore, doctors are not penalized financially by serving in the rural settings. Newly graduated doctors do two years of community service in the countryside before going on to residencies or specialization. Many doctors have served overseas in Angola, South Africa, Nicaragua, Kampuchea, and other places.

Cuba has also offered medical care to the children of Chernobyl, Ukraine, who were victims of the nuclear reactor explosion on April 26, 1986. In March 1990 the first planeload of 139 children and parents arrived for treatment at the Pioneer Youth camp on the Isle of Youth, and since then 13,000 Ukrainian children have been treated there.

In 1983 Cuba began a series of measures to detect and control acquired immune deficiency syndrome (AIDS). It banned imports of blood-derived products from countries with reported cases of AIDS, established sixty laboratories connected to blood banks, and tested Cubans who had returned from overseas service. Thirteen sanatoriums were established both to prevent an epidemic and to provide immediate care for patients. An out-patient care system, established in 1993, includes counseling by social workers to families of patients and help in finding work, housing, boarding schools, or day-care centers for children. Such patients have the right to maintain their job or salary.

When the U.S. blockade of Cuba was first established, it allowed Cuba to obtain foodstuffs and medical supplies by sale or trade. But on May 14, 1964, this exemption was ended. Since then, through the Torricelli and

Helms-Burton laws (see below), the United States has sought to prevent both U.S. subsidiaries and companies in other countries from sending food and medical supplies to Cuba, even though such policy is in violation of international law and basic human rights. For example, Medix (Argentina), Dow (Italy), and Toshiba (Japan) were refused licenses to sell medical equipment to Cuba. CGR Thomas (Germany) was denied a license to sell Cuba spare parts for X-ray equipment. Dow (Italy) was refused permission to sell water-treatment resins, and Eli Lilly Canada was prevented from selling its medicines to Cuba. As a result there has been a troubling increase in mortality from infectious diseases and the lack of hospital equipment and in low-birth-weight babies.

Improved Status of Women. The revolution marked a profound watershed in Cuban history in terms of the position of women. Before 1959 a number of women had played important roles in the struggle for independence: Ana Betancourt (who participated in the First War for Independence and called for equal rights for women) Mariana Grajales Coello (mother of Antonio Maceo), Haydée Santamaria, Melba Hernandez, Celia Sánchez, Vilma Espin, and others who were leaders in the 26 July Movement. Most women, however, were subject to men rather than in control of their own destiny. Their lives centered on their homes. Less than 10 percent worked outside their homes, and of these, 70 percent worked as domestic servants; the other 30 percent were teachers, nurses, secretaries, or laborers in tobacco or textile factories. Women from poor rural areas increasingly migrated to the cities, especially Havana, trying to find work there. Many of them ended up as prostitutes catering to North American tourists, businessmen, and military personnel.

In the revolutionary struggle, however, women all over the island gave background support to the 26 July Movement, organizing demonstrations, collecting supplies for the rebels, sewing uniforms, hiding guerrillas in their homes, and serving as messengers and spies. Soon after the triumph of the revolution, in August 1960 they organized the Federation of Cuban Women with Vilma Espin as director.

One of the federation's first tasks was setting up schools for peasant women—for maids whose employers had left for the United States and for prostitutes whose clientele had gone—to train them as child-care workers and office personnel. Another early task was establishing day-care centers around the island for children between six months and six years. These centers, open from early morning until after work, are housed in some of the mansions left behind by rich émigrés or increasingly, in new buildings built specifically for them. The children are provided with clothes, nutritious meals, regular medical examinations, shots, and dental care. They learn basic skills such as how to count, tell time, and handle arguments peacefully. The staff is made up of university-trained administrators and teachers, a medical team, culinary and maintenance personnel, and parental volunteers. The centers were originally free; now there is a small charge scaled to the parents' salary.

In 1974 the federation was instrumental in getting a Maternity Rights law passed. It provides for eighteen weeks of paid leave—six weeks before birth and twelve weeks after—with eighteen additional days off for medical checkups for mother and baby. The law also permits a mother to take a year's unpaid leave and still return to her former job.

In 1975, after considerable grass-roots discussion, a Family Code was passed. Marriage means "equal rights and duties for both parties." Both spouses must cooperate in bringing up the children according to the principles of socialist morality and participate in running the home. The children are obliged to respect and obey their parents. Parents are to support and educate their children. Divorce and alimony are also regulated.

Cuban women have the right to abortion on demand, free of charge. However, because of an excellent sex education program in the schools, the easy accessibility of cheap contraceptives, and the strong social and economic support for women (equal pay for equal work, free health care, and educational opportunities) the abortion rate has declined.

Machismo, so prevalent throughout Latin America, is less strong in Cuba because of the consciousness-raising that has gone on since 1959. Nevertheless, it is still alive in many homes where the working wife or mother is burdened with a second job of being the sole (or main) person responsible for shopping, cooking, and housework.

Reduced Racial Prejudice. In a speech in March 1959 Fidel Castro denounced racial discrimination in the most sweeping terms. He criticized the discrimination in recreation areas and in private education and the unwritten barriers that prevented blacks from full equality of access to jobs. Accordingly, in April the government desegregated all the beaches in Cuba. In October it nationalized and desegregated all private schools. As Lourdes Casal has pointed out in "Race Relations in Contemporary Cuba" (in *The Cuba Reader*), "It was Fidel Castro's role to be the first Cuban white ruler to recognize openly the mulatto character of Cuban culture and nationhood. When in his speech of 19 April 1976 he quietly asserted 'we are Latin African people,' Fidel was making history" (p. 484).

Today racial discrimination has officially been eliminated from jobs, education, and social facilities, and the egalitarian and redistributive measures of the revolution (such as the Agrarian and Urban Reform Laws) and the equalization of access to the health and educational systems have radically changed Cuban society for the benefit of blacks. Today more blacks in Cuba own their homes than in any other country of the world (Casal, in *The Cuba Reader*, Brenner, p. 482).

Encouragement of Cuban Culture. After 1959 the government made special efforts to develop the cultural resources of the nation: theaters, orchestras, choruses, drama groups, ballet and modern dance groups, artists, and film makers. The members of these groups receive a salary from the state for their full-time work, which includes serving as

The revolution has ended official race discrimination. This is a member of the Young Pioneers, a Cuban equivalent of the Boy Scouts and Girl Scouts.

teachers and giving free (or minimal-cost) concerts. The National Ballet Company, founded by Alicia Alonso, the National Chorus of Cuba, directed by Digna Guerra, and other artistic groups are known the world over.

Very soon after 1959 the government established art galleries in small towns, to make art accessible to the citizens. The National Museum of Fine Arts in Havana was expanded to include the whole range of Cuban art from colonial portraiture and scenery to impressionistic and abstract art. Special museums, e.g. featuring African art and sculpture or the painting of the Ecuadoran artist Oswaldo Guayasamín, were inaugurated.

Film had an important part in the cultural life of the nation—documentaries such as those by Santiago Alvarez (the "Chronicler of the Third World") and Estela Bravo and full-length films have helped the nation to reach a new degree of understanding and sensitivity to contemporary issues. The award-winning *Strawberry and Chocolate,* about a heterosexual young man in the Young Communists and a homosexual, who meet in the Coppelia ice cream center in Havana, brought about a profound change in the way Cubans view homosexuality. It has also been shown in the United States.

Music is one of the most popular Cuban pastimes. Musicians are educated by the state and are paid a state salary. In the 1990s performance groups such as Charango Habanera have been encouraged to tour in Europe to earn hard currency.

Town libraries are kept open late into the evening to give workers a chance to use them. Workers and students, old and young, flock to Coppelia ice cream centers located in almost every town. In Havana the Coppelia takes up a whole city block. Crowds also watch free baseball games (a national sport in Cuba), which are the occasion for intense inter-city rivalries.

In Cuba one is never far from the sound of music—musicians with guitars, maracas, claves, and drums playing rumba, mambo, salsa, and Afro-Cuban rhythms on the radio or in local bars and cafes. The larger cities have Old and New Trova Houses (where singers and musicians offer either traditional or modern songs), cabarets that host excellent musical groups, and nightclubs such as the Tropicana that offer spectacular musical and dance shows.

Economic Development

Cuba faced massive problems in the areas of housing and employment. Che Guevarra, as head of the Central Planning Board and minister of the Department of Industry (see box), believed that they could be solved only by reorganizing the economy according to socialist principles.

More Housing. After 1959 the government passed a law that allowed families that had more than one house to keep only one. It turned large houses (especially in Miramar and other richer sections of Havana) that were abandoned in the early years of the revolution by émigré families into apartment houses or schools, day-care centers, offices, or embassies. The worst slum housing in Havana was replaced by new apartment buildings, but rather than continue the pre-1959 pattern of granting most of the construction budget to the capital, the government gave the countryside priority. Havana was eventually to have its turn, but by then, construction materials were in short supply because of the blockade. Visitors often comment about the ruinous condition of buildings in Havana, but what sets this scene off from similar scenes in other Latin American cities is the good health and high educational level of the inhabitants.

The "Heroic Guerrilla"

In 1960 Alberto Korda took a photo of Che Guevara in a beret with a star on it, attending the funeral for the victims of the sabotage bombing of the Belgian supply ship *La Coubre*. That picture of the "Heroic Guerrilla" eventually became a popular icon reproduced in painting, murals, posters, jewelry, and on T-shirts all over Cuba.

Ernesto Guevara was born in Argentina in 1928 and studied medicine there. In 1952 he began to travel around Latin America on a motorcycle. While in Peru, he treated patients in

Theodore A. Braun

Che Guevara, hero of the revolution and a model for Cuban youth, appears on murals like this one in Havana and posters all over Cuba.

a leper colony. He returned to Argentina to finish his medical training, becoming a doctor in 1953, and then began traveling again. In 1954 he was in Guatemala when a CIA-backed coup deposed the government—a radicalizing experience for him.

In 1955 he was in Mexico, where he met Fidel Castro and his rebel band and immediately joined them. They gave him the nickname "Che," an Argentine term of greeting. The next year he sailed to Cuba with them on the *Granma* and was one of the dozen survivors to escape from Batista forces into the Sierra Maestra. There in the mountains he had a further radicalizing experience living among the peasants, coming face to face with what he called the "marks of the Sierra Maestra"—prematurely aged and toothless women and children with distended bellies, parasites, rickets, and general vitamin deficiency.

As one of the chief commanders of Castro's rebel forces, Che was known for his visionary intelligence, integrity, sincerity, Spartan living habits, and hard work. After the triumph of the revolution in 1959, he was declared a Cuban citizen in recognition of his contribution to Cuba's liberation. Although he served as president of the National Bank, director of the Central Planning Board, and minister of the Department of Industry, he continued to give many hours of voluntary service in the cane fields and mines and on construction projects.

Che, as he was known to all Cubans, was convinced that the participation of the politically aware workers was the key to the reorganization of Cuban society. He constantly emphasized moral values as the foundation of this new society, moral incentives for work, and the value of voluntary service. True socialism, he said, is a product of consciousness, not just of economic production. He was critical of the Soviet Union's emphasis on material incentives and its reliance on a rigid, vertical bureaucracy.

He was also a strong internationalist. There can be no socialism, he said, if there is not a change in consciousness that translates into a new fraternal attitude toward humanity. "There are no borders in this struggle to the death, we cannot be indifferent to what is happening in any part of the world; a victory of ours . . . is victory for all."

In his later years, Che took part in revolutionary struggle in the Belgian Congo and Bolivia. He was captured and killed by Bolivian forces with CIA help in 1967 (Franklin, *Cuba and the United States*, p. 84). Che has become one of the primary role models for the Cuban children and youth. His life and values are recalled and given special honor throughout Cuba.

∿∿ ∿∿ ∿∿ ∿∿ ∿∿ ∿∿ ∿∿ ∿∿ ∿∿ ∿∿ ∿∿ ∿∿ ∿∿ ∿∿ ∿∿
∿∿ ∿∿ ∿∿ ∿∿ ∿∿ ∿∿ ∿∿ ∿∿ ∿∿ ∿∿ ∿∿ ∿∿ ∿∿ ∿∿ ∿∿

Outside Havana, however, one can find new towns such as Alamar housing the city's overflow. The five-story apartment buildings (the maximum height so that elevators are not needed) containing apartments of varying size are built in clusters around a market, cultural center, theater, swimming pool, and family doctor.

New housing clusters on a smaller scale have been constructed all over the island, often by cooperative farms, factories, ministries, or organizations. In earlier years, if the government built them, the rent was 10 percent of the salary of the main wage earner in the family; if the factory or farm was the builder, then the rent was only 6 percent. The new housing law of 1984 turned all renters into owners, making mortgage payments at 2 to 3 percent over twenty years. Farmers were permitted to remain in their thatched houses or could move. Even the most humble hut, however, was electrified so that it could have a television set.

Cuba provided labor for this construction process through microbrigades of volunteer workers (especially those in need of housing). They took leaves of one or more years to work in the brigades, while their former employers continued to pay their salaries, and their fellow workers worked harder or overtime without increased pay. The government paid for the materials and supplied architects, engineers, plumbers, electricians, and other advisers. Housing was usually assigned by need or merit, 80 percent by labor unions, and 20 percent by the government. The microbrigade movement lasted from 1971 to 1978. It was severely criticized for a monotonous prefabricated building style that was incompatible with living traditions in the countryside; faulty work by volunteers, who

William C. Winslow

City mansions abandoned by rich émigrés were taken over by the government for schools, offices, or apartments. Many are crumbling for lack of building materials.

The government has built large modern apartment houses, especially in the country, using volunteer labor brigades.

were often paid more than regular construction workers; and the exclusion of some people with the greatest housing need—people without jobs, such as old age pensioners and single mothers.

In 1986, as a result of the government's program to rectify past mistakes and new emphasis on voluntary service, the microbrigade program was revitalized but placed under local rather than national supervision, which offered more flexible architectural approaches. Since then, microbrigade projects have expanded far beyond housing to include child-care centers, schools for the handicapped, polyclinics, buildings for family doctors, offices, schools, and bakeries. A similar program of social microbrigades, made up of workers who live in the same neighborhood, repair or renovate existing housing. These brigades are also helping to solve the growing problem of unemployment due to the embargo. Despite these efforts, the housing situation, especially in the cities, is still critical. Because of the lack of building materials due to the embargo, work on new and restored housing has greatly slowed. Several families and generations have had to crowd together, a situation that often creates stress.

More Employment. When the state nationalized all property and thus became the primary employer and landlord, Cuban employment changed radically. Middle-class Cubans who had been working in private enterprises, whether Cuban- or foreign-owned, found their jobs gone. Employment in law, insurance, real estate, rent collection, travel, gambling, and brokerage firms had vanished. Many Cubans who had lost these jobs became early emigrants to the United States.

Of the population that remained, at first almost everyone had a job as part of the government's effort to eliminate unemployment, especially during the dead season. Some of these jobs were nonessential, such as running self-operating hotel elevators, and untrained workers were not always efficient. A new salary grid was instituted with a salary spread from 95 pesos to 700 pesos. There was no difference in pay between men and women for the same job. Every worker received a month of paid vacation each year. To make life even more equitable, the government rationed basic foods and clothing, which sold at very low prices. Those with special needs, such as children and the elderly, were given special allotments of milk and other beneficial products. For many years there were also parallel stores carrying food and clothing that were free of rationing but sold at higher prices.

When U.S. currency was legalized in 1992, the salary system was greatly skewed. Since US $1.00 was worth 20 Cuban pesos in 1998, Cubans who can earn tourist dollars or who receive aid from relatives in the United States have a tremendous advantage over other Cubans.

A New Economic System. The revolutionary government, inspired especially by Che Guevarra, had a vision of forming a New Man and a New Society—a society that would forswear material incentives and individual self-interest in favor of moral incentives and the common interest. At first the government hoped to offer free utilities, free local bus transportation, and free local telephone service, as well as free education and health care. And it hoped to diversify the sugar-based economy. But because of the exodus of so many technicians, professionals, and managers; the opposition of the United States; and their own inexperience in economic development and central planning, their early efforts to organize the economy were improvised rather than thought through. The government set up a threefold agricultural structure—state farms for the larger sugar plantations, cooperative farms that gave farmers access to better housing and more sophisticated machinery, and individual farms for those peasant farmers who wanted keep working their small farms with oxen.

The U.S. trade embargo and the ending of the sugar quota in 1961 brought a crisis situation. The offer of the Soviet Union to pick up the sugar quota at higher than world prices, and further offers of trade and aid, saved the day for Cuba and saved the revolution. In the years between 1959 and 1970 exports to the Soviet Union increased from 12.9 million pesos to 529 million pesos, and imports went from zero to 686 million pesos.

But with this valuable Soviet assistance came a Soviet model of socialism that was not Cuban—a static, hierarchical, dogmatic model that used authoritarian central planning, a bureaucratic mindset, intellectual intolerance, and an ideology of controlling nature and society. It led the Cuban planners into many errors, which Castro's rectification process of 1986 was designed to correct and which indeed saved Cuba from a collapse similar to that of the Soviet Communist system in 1989.

Political Development

The revolutionary government, as it developed structures enabling participatory democracy, had to guard against hostility both inside and outside the country.

Neighborhood Committees. In response to intensified counterrevolutionary attacks and sabotage, in September 1960 Castro challenged Cubans to form Committees for the Defense of the Revolution (CDR), made up of residents on one side of a neighborhood block, to guard public buildings, patrol the streets at night, and protect the neighborhood against sabotage and petty theft. The nighttime patrol was carried out by a pair of women up to midnight and a pair of men after midnight—neighbors taking a turn once a month. Very soon, these block organizations began to incorporate activities beyond vigilance—making sure children and older people had

Members of a block organization, called a Committee for the Defense of the Revolution, meet monthly to discuss local problems. They provide security and encourage conservation, school attendance, health programs, and local clean-up.

inoculations and vaccines; supervising blood donation drives and voluntary neighborhood clean-up on Sunday morning; encouraging conservation of electricity and water, recycling, and celebration of national holidays; maintaining contact with residents in overseas service; and making sure there was no truancy from school.

In a sense, these block organizations became *koinonia* (fellowship) groups, whose members developed a sense of caring and responsibility for one another. Many church members have been in the CDRs. Ebenezer Baptist Church in Havana for a while changed its Sunday service from the morning to the evening so more of its members could participate in the Sunday morning neighborhood clean-up. Vigilance by the CDRs has made it safe for women to walk alone in the streets at any hour of the night. To celebrate the national CDR anniversary each September, the members of each CDR place a big kettle over a fire in their street. Then each family brings some meat or vegetables for *caldosa*, a thick, nourishing stew that everyone eats during the evening celebration of speeches, dancing, and other refreshments.

Because of the CDRs, the Federation of Cuban Women, and the social concern developed throughout Cuban society, there are virtually no lost or runaway children or homeless men or women on the streets, very little violent crime, and few unwilling social outsiders.

People's Power. The governmental structure through which Cubans participate in their democracy is called *Poder Popular* (People's Power). At the bottom, several CDRs join together to form a zone. Each zone chooses among people nominated by that zone and by trade unions, women's groups and other mass organizations, delegates to the 169 municipal assemblies, the 14 provincial assemblies, and the National Assembly. Nominees have their photo and biography publicized and speak at zone meetings but are not allowed to spend any money in running for office. They are chosen by secret ballot with members of the Pioneer Youth observing the counting of votes. Participation in elections usually runs about 95 percent.

Serving in municipal and provincial assemblies (two and a half years) and the National Assembly (five years) is not a full-time job; delegates continue their normal occupations. They report regularly to zone meetings or assemblies, where citizens can question them and recall them if so desired. New laws or changes in old ones are discussed at zone meetings and also in CDRs, workplaces, and other key places; reactions and recommendations are sent back up the ladder.

The 589-member National Assembly, which includes three evangelical pastors, Raúl Suárez of Ebenezer Baptist Church in Havana, Sergio

Arce of the Presbyterian Church in Varadaro, and Odén Marichal, president of the Cuban Council of Churches, meets twice a year. The National Assembly elects a 31-member Council of State, an on-going executive committee. Fidel Castro is president both of the Council of State and of the government. He nominates a 44-member Council of Ministers, who must be confirmed by the National Assembly.

Castro, like Martí, has been called the Mentor of Cuba. In his early speeches he explained situations, interpreted events, and offered criticism and hope. He is constantly on the move around the island, talking to people, sounding out public opinion, hearing criticism, and accepting suggestions. People know him as a person who listens, who has a tremendous intellectual curiosity, who speaks candidly, who does not hesitate to admit making mistakes; they feel they can trust him to tell the truth.

Fidel Castro, in army uniform, moves about the country giving speeches and listening to citizens. Here he visits the Methodist church in Vedado in 1984, his first church appearance since 1959.

Castro has many times said that he has less power than the U.S. president (in terms of being able to start a war or take other actions that commit the nation). His main power derives from his moral and historical authority, his interpretive abilities, his sensitivity to those on the underside of history, his oratorical talents, and his charisma. When he passes from the scene, no one will be able to take his place. His brother Raúl is the designated successor, but young men such as Ricardo Alarcón, Roberto Robaina, and Carlos Lage, could give able leadership. An exile who wanted to succeed Castro was Jorge Mas Canosa (see chapter 4).

Communist Party. The Communist Party is the only political party in Cuba. It was formed in October 1965 out of the merger of three groups—the 26 July Movement, the 13 March Revolutionary Directorate, and the Popular Socialist Party (founded in 1925). Its function is not to support candidates for election but to serve as the moral guide to the revolution. At the grass-roots level, prospective members (who are considered model citizens) are nominated by their workplaces or other organizations. If the party judges them suitable, they are given an invitation to join, which they can accept or reject. The party holds a congress every five years, when it evaluates the progress and problems of the nation and chooses its Central Committee, which in turn chooses the twenty-six-member Political Bureau. At the top of both the People's Power and Communist Party structures, the personnel tend to merge. Fidel Castro is not only president of the Council of State but also First Secretary of the party. Both structures are in the tradition of José Martí and other Cuban nationalists, which may help to explain why Cuba has been able to withstand both U.S. antipathy and the Soviet collapse.

The U.S. government and the Cuban exiles want Cuba to allow political parties that sponsor candidates, as in the United States. That would give the United States an easier chance to penetrate the Cuban electoral process with U.S. ideas, money, and candidates, as happened in the last two campaigns in Nicaragua and as various interests do in the United States. Cuba views the two major U.S. parties as wings of a single, business-controlled party. It also sees an important distinction between representative democracy (the U.S. system) and participatory democracy, evidenced by popular involvement in the political process (as in Cuba).

Human Rights. Cuba has put great emphasis on the social and economic rights listed in the UN Universal Declaration of Human rights. The Cuban Constitution guarantees that

Everyone who is able to work has the opportunity to have a job with which to contribute to the good of society . . . , including equal pay for equal work, a weekly rest period, and an annual paid vacation.
Everyone has the right to free health protection and care.
Everyone has the right to an education free of charge, and no child is left without schooling, food, and clothing.
Everyone has the right to physical education, sports, and recreation.
It is working to achieve that no family is left without a comfortable place to live.

Cuba has made tremendous progress in seeing that these basic social and economic rights are realized. But critics have continued to raise concerns about the more individualistic and political human rights set forth in the UN declaration, such as the rights to freedom of thought and religion; freedom of opinion and expression; and freedom of peaceful assembly.

Castro has frequently said, "Within the Revolution—everything, against the Revolution, nothing." He himself has taken the lead in criticiz-

Children first is a policy of the revolutionary government. The state provides inexpensive day-care centers for children of working parents and special milk rations.

ing mistakes and corruption within the revolution. Many avenues of popular criticism, including criticism of Castro, have been established—through the CDRs, the Women's Federation, labor unions, other mass organizations, and special hearings. The test, of course, comes in distinguishing between what is intended to correct and improve the revolution and what is intended to weaken and destroy it.

The Cuban Constitution guarantees freedom of speech and of the press within the objectives of socialist society. Most countries, however, have limited this freedom in times of war. Since 1959, and especially in the mid-1960s, Cuba has been under intensive overt and covert attack, from the United States and from dissident Cubans, including some church leaders, who wanted to bring Cuba back into political and economic alignment with the United States. The United States not only encouraged the Bay of Pigs invasion of 1961 but planned sabotage and other destabilizing events, as will be discussed later. The Catholic hierarchy and many conservative Evangelicals, fearing an atheistic government as well as suffering the loss of schools and hospitals, openly opposed the revolution. Cuba's survival was not a sure thing, so any kind of dissidence, real or imaginary, was quickly penalized, often without what the United States would consider due process of law. (During World Wars I and II and the cold war, the United States kept a close eye on German Americans, Japanese Americans, reputed Communists, and any others it considered a threat to national security and curtailed political criticism and dissidence.)

In November 1963 Cuba instituted obligatory military service for all male citizens between seventeen and forty-five. In 1965 the government established Military Units to Aid Production (UMAP)—a program for recruits not considered politically trustworthy. Channeled into forced labor in the cane fields were various kinds of "dissidents," "social deviants," homosexuals, and conservative Catholic and Protestant clergy. The UMAP program, however, came under such heavy Cuban criticism that it was ended in 1967.

Although the Communist government has never forbidden worship or Christian education within church walls, it refused churches access to newspapers, radio, and television and the right to hold public processions and gatherings in public places such as stadiums. In 1965 it arrested many of the ministers in the Western Baptist Convention, tried them, and found them guilty of espionage. It accused members of the Jehovah's Witnesses and Seventh Day Adventists of being counterrevolutionary because they refused to enter the army, salute the national flag, and work on Sundays. For a while they were jailed but later on, ignored.

Counterrevolutionary groups have used the human-rights issue as a cover for their counterrevolutionary activity, and U.S. administrations have consistently made the "repression" of human rights a central aspect of their ideological war against Cuba. In this conflict, the issue of "freedom" often crowds out issues of "equality," "democracy," and "justice," that ought to be part of the dialogue.

As Tony Platt and Ed McCaughan write in their "Human Rights in Cuba: Politics and Ideology" (in *Transformation and Struggle: Cuba Faces the 1990s*, 1990, edited by Sandor Halebsky and John M. Kirk):

> The U.S human rights campaign against Cuba has been constructed on cold war mythologies and demonic imagery of holy war rather than facts and informed debate. . . .
>
> In its assessments of human rights in Cuba, the United States appears locked within a worldview that values individual liberties more than collective rights and stresses procedure over substantive contents.
>
> Such a perspective ignores advances made by non-Western states and social movements, and even its Western allies, to expand the traditional liberal notions of rights so as to include economic and subsistence rights, social and cultural rights, and, perhaps most significantly, people's collective rights, including the primary right to self-determination. . . .
>
> The United States and other Western powers have historically been reluctant to give much weight to peoples' rights. Indeed, in its active efforts to block Third World attempts to assert self-determination, the United States has frequently used "a self-serving rhetoric of human rights" to justify its overt interventions, Cuba being a prime example. (pp. 73, 75)

As long as the revolutionary government was struggling for survival, it felt it had to keep a close watch lest full expression of political rights endanger its life. Although its existence is now recognized as legitimate by most people in Cuba and by most of the rest of the world, it still finds itself in a situation of war and fears to relax too far its degree of political control. Thus there are still reports of dissenting journalists and members of various unofficial dissenting groups being harassed, arrested, imprisoned, and losing their jobs (Amnesty International, *Cuba: Silencing the Voices of Dissent*, Dec. 1992; "Inside Cuba's Gulag," *World Press Review*, July 1998). Others have been imprisoned for trying to leave Cuba without permission. Amnesty International estimated about three hundred to five hundred of such political prisoners of conscience in 1992 plus as many more imprisoned for terrorism and sabotage. Many may not have been fairly tried, and prison conditions are often poor. (Although the United States is not in a similar situation, the spectrum of political expression is limited in terms of representation on panels and in public analysis.)

Foreign Relations. During these thirty years Cuba's foreign policy was marked principally by enmity toward the United States and friendship toward the Soviet Union and Eastern bloc. In addition, Cuba established close relationships with various countries in Africa and the Caribbean that have black populations—Angola, Ethiopia, South Africa, Mozambique, Tanzania, Algeria, Sierra Leona, Grenada, and Jamaica.

In Angola, shortly before the date set for independence, November 11, 1975, when a transitional government representing three parties was to be set up, South Africa invaded Angola to give support to two of them. The third sent an SOS to Cuba, which sent 25,000 volunteer troops to Angola, forcing South Africa to withdraw its troops to the border. Twelve years later when South African and mercenary forces began to advance from Namibia into Angola, Cuba sent 300,000 troops and in a decisive battle at Cuito Cuanavale, forced South Africa to withdraw completely from Angola, and set in motion plans for the independence of Namibia.

In South Africa, the "white flight" that accompanied the first nonracial elections in 1994 left more than two thousand vacant posts for doctors—most of them in rural areas. Cuba sent Cuban doctors, of which it had a large supply, to help fill those posts, 359 of them since 1996. The doctors, who sign three-year contracts, are paid by South Africa. Cuba has also supplied many technical workers and doctors to more than forty countries, such as Chile, Mexico, El Salvador, Nicaragua, Honduras, Kampuchea, South Yemen, Syria, and Laos.

One of the most grating points of contention between Cuba and the United States is the U.S. base at Guantánamo Bay. The perpetual lease of this land to the United States was part of a treaty forced upon Cuba in 1903. According to the Vienna Convention on the Law of Treaties, a treaty is void if it was produced by the threat or use of force. Therefore, Cubans consider the U.S. base a breach of international law and a denial of Cuban sovereignty. The Cuban government has refused to cash the $4,055 U.S. rent checks. The use of the Guantánamo base became even more of an emotional issue in 1994 and 1995 when Cuban émigrés were incarcerated in concentration camps on the base.

Religious Development

The revolution, especially after Castro declared it socialist, caught both Catholics and Evangelicals by surprise. Both groups had become accustomed to belonging to a capitalist society and to providing needed social services. The loss of their schools to nationalization came as a great shock to both. Many church members and clergy, feeling that they were now living in enemy (or at least hostile) territory, left for the United States. Conservative Catholics took militant action against the government and developed closer ties with counterrevolutionary, anticommunist forces in the United States. Finally in September 1961 the Cuban government expelled 132 Spanish priests, sending them back to Spain. Church members who remained in Cuba often felt they were living in a strange new land with different ground rules. Because of opposition from more conservative churchmen, the government blocked Christian students from entering careers in psychology, the political sciences, journalism, and diplomacy.

But soon a new situation began to unfold. As Christians who remained in Cuba began to see the hungry being fed, the naked being clothed, the poor being lifted up (all of it by the government, outside the aegis of the church), they were filled with surprise. Here was God fulfilling the prayers and aims of the church through the instrument of a secular "Cyrus." But there was a big difference—the needs of all the people were now being solved by structural changes in society, not the needs of individuals by Christian charity. That brought a new question to challenge the church: What was its mission if there were no longer poor people to help? The answer came down to the basic hermeneutical calling of the church: to interpret what God is doing in the world and to join God there. Thus Christians began to take an increasingly active role in revolutionary society. They joined CDRs and unions, served in local government, and did volunteer work—even though certain careers, avenues of public communication, and membership in the party and the upper echelon of government were closed to them. In some of these activities they met members of the

Afro-Cuban syncretistic religions, who had immediately felt the benefits of the revolution and given it their support. The experiences of Ysel Perez (see box) are an example of Evangelical Cuban Christians who came to terms with the revolution.

~~~ ~~~ ~~~ ~~~ ~~~ ~~~ ~~~ ~~~ ~~~ ~~~ ~~~ ~~~ ~~~ ~~~ ~~~
~~~ ~~~ ~~~ ~~~ ~~~ ~~~ ~~~ ~~~ ~~~ ~~~ ~~~ ~~~ ~~~ ~~~ ~~~

A Pro-revolutionary Cuban Christian

Ysel Pérez, a middle-class Evangelical Cuban who did not emigrate, was born in 1919 in Oriente Province, the daughter of a mechanic in a sugar mill. The family moved to Cienfugeos, where her father became a mechanic for the Cuban Electric Power Company. After beginning in a public primary school, Ysel was given a scholarship by Methodist missionaries enabling her to attend Methodist primary and secondary schools.

At eighteen, she married Orlando Rovira, an accountant in the Cuban Electric Power Company. They had two sons, Orlando and René. In 1950 Ysel's husband was transferred to the head office in Havana. There they became active in the Miguel A. Soto Methodist Church. During the Batista dictatorship from 1952 to 1959, when Batista was killing many young people suspected of opposition, Ysel worried whenever their two teenage sons left their apartment and breathed a sigh of relief when they returned safely. Almost everyone they knew wanted a different government but didn't know what could be done.

Then, thanks to Fidel and his rebels, they became free of Batista. It was a special moment for the whole country, for which people were very grateful. No one knew much about Fidel, but when he spoke in the plaza, people enjoyed listening to him, and they came to know and trust him as a person of honesty and integrity with the best interests of Cuba at heart. Many called him El Caballo (The Horse) because of his strength.

But when Fidel declared the revolution socialist, many Cubans were frightened of the unknown future. Believing that they couldn't live without the North American way, many left for the United States. Many Methodists left, too. The church didn't have leaders or members who understood the revolution. Out of ten thousand, only two thousand to three thousand remained, and out of a hundred pastors (all part of the Florida Methodist Conference), only five stayed in Cuba. The sons, Orlando and René, were so disappointed by this exodus that they stopped going to church.

Then something remarkable began to happen. The remaining church members discovered that the goals of the revolution and the goals of the church were very much alike—that the revolution was trying to do what the church had been trying to do for many years. They could see that something better was coming to the nation, and they began to read the Bible in a new way. Why couldn't God be in the middle of this changing situation? they wondered.

One of the lessons the revolution was teaching the church was its way of trying to solve the misery of the Cuban people—not only by giving charity at Christmas but in changing the economic system. As Ysel said, "Our family was better off financially before 1959 and paid a price, but I'm happier now because the larger part of the Cuban people are better off now."

Ysel served for twenty-two years as public health coordinator for their CDR, making sure that the children received vaccinations and all the women received pap tests. She taught also in church school, was an elder in their local church, and was national president of Methodist Church Women. Orlando served as church school teacher, treasurer, and lay preacher and was treasurer of the Ecumenical Council of Cuba before his death in 1979. The couple's younger son René, a mechanic, took part in the national literacy drive as a teacher. He and his elder brother, Orlando, a geologist, gave voluntary service in Ethiopia.

Today Ysel lives in the family apartment with René, her daughter-in-law Miriam (a Marxist professor with the Federation of Cuban Women), and granddaughter Yeni (a recently baptized Methodist and a member of the Young Communists). It is a family of great love and solidarity. Ysel says,

It has been a great privilege for me to live this experience before and after the triumph of the revolution. It has often been hard because of the blockade, but we have learned to live without many things we lived with before. The revolution is trying to do the best for the whole nation. It's not heaven here, but neither is it hell.

We live in great hope. We see God present in all the spheres of life. The revolution has helped us read the Bible in a new way, and to think through what we believed. Jesus Christ came to change things in history, and paid for change with his life. And so we pay, too, for change. This is an important time for the church in Cuba. People are now returning to the church, recognizing a need for more spirituality in their lives. And the revolution at this moment is expectant of the church, waiting for the church to be the church.

The following years were ones of great theological ferment. Although largely isolated from the liberation theology that blossomed in the rest of Latin America, Cuban churches, out of their encounter with socialist values, began to forge a new theological understanding. The Ecumenical Council of Cuba encouraged Marxist-Christian dialogue and ecumenical activities within the churches, and the World Council of Churches served, with the blessing of the U.S. and Cuban governments, as an intermediary for the transfer of funds from the U.S. to Cuban churches.

In 1977 the Presbyterian-Reformed Church of Cuba, after much local discussion, adopted a new Confession of Faith, which viewed work as a principle of human spirituality and salvation as the socioeconomic and ecological, as well as spiritual, reconstruction of the human being. In 1978 *Cristo Vivo en Cuba* (Christ Lives in Cuba) was published, the theological reflections of six Cuban church leaders (Sergio Arce Martínez, Adolfo Ham Reyes, Uxmal Livio, Díaz Rodriguez, Israel Batista Guerra, and Juan Ramón de La Paz Cerezo). It was followed later by a series of books that focused on evangelism and politics, the church and revolution, theology in revolution, and Christian-Marxist unity. A number of theological journals were published regularly.

Meanwhile, the Cuban government was making a concerted effort to foster harmonious church-state relations. In 1979 Dr. José Felipe Carneado, head of the Religious Affairs Office, visited the annual assembly of the Ecumenical Council of Cuba for the first time, and since then, his office has been in a close and friendly relationship to the church. Fidel Castro visited progressive churches in Chile in 1971, Jamaica in 1977, and Nicaragua in 1980. In 1984 with Jesse Jackson, he attended a Martin Luther King colloquium in the Vedado Methodist Church (his first visit to a Cuban church since 1959) and gave an eight-minute talk that was televised nationally. The next year, 2 million copies of *Fidel y la Religion* (1986) (based on twenty-three hours of interviews by Frei Betto, a Brazilian priest) were printed and sold by the Cuban government—an astonishing development that opened up much new interest in the church in Cuba. In it Castro made the following important remarks:

> I believe that from the political point of view, religion is not in itself an opiate or a miraculous remedy. It may become an opiate or a wonderful cure if it is used or applied to defend oppressors and exploiters or the oppressed and the exploited, depending on the approach adopted toward the political, social, or material problems of human beings who, aside from theology or religious belief, are born and must live in this world.
>
> From a strictly political point of view—and I think I know something about politics—I believe that it is possible for Christians to be Marxists as well and to work together with Marxist communists to transform the world. The important thing is that in both cases they be honest revolutionaries who want to end the exploitation of man by man and to struggle for a fair distribution of social wealth, equality, fraternity, and the dignity of all human beings—that is, that they be standard-bearers of the most advanced political, economic, and social ideas, even though in the case of the Christians their starting point is a religious concept. (p .235)

In 1986 Ebenezer Baptist Church in Havana and two other Baptist churches were expelled from the Southern Baptist Convention in the United States for engaging in ecumenical activities alien to the church, for elevating women to positions of equality in the church, for finding signs of the Kingdom of God in Cuban social development, for youth immorality (dancing), and for heresy. In 1989, after a three-year period of study and meetings, nine progressive Cuban Baptist churches formed the Fraternity of Baptist Churches of Cuba. They affirmed the following principles: the local independence of the church, freedom of conscience, the universal priesthood of believers (rejecting all types of paternalism and clericalism), separation of church and state, recognition of the role of women in the life of the church as co-equal to that of men, an ecumenical attitude to the different branches of Christianity, study of the Bible including the social dimension of the gospel, and liturgical renovation with elements of Cubanness. The fraternity now has forty churches and missions in it.

Ebenezer Baptist Church, in Havana, through its Martin Luther King, Jr., Memorial Center, offers programs in theology, lay education, communications, and housing renovation. It is a reception point for shipments of humanitarian supplies from U.S. religious groups.

In 1989 the Council of Churches of Cuba (formerly the Ecumenical Council) published a new ecumenical hymnal, *Toda la Iglesia Canta* (The Whole Church Sings). The editor was Lois Kroehler, national director of music of the Presbyterian-Reformed Church of Cuba, a U.S. missionary who had been serving in Cuba since 1949.

Another important event was a six-hour dialogue on the relationship between the government and the church between some sixty Evangelical leaders and Fidel Castro on April 2, 1990. Once again Castro affirmed, "What should divide us is not if one is a believer or not; what we should ask ourselves is whether we are revolutionaries or not." The uncut dialogue was shown twice on national television and put into a video. One result of this process of rapprochement came in October 1991, when Communist Party membership was opened up to revolutionary Christians and other religious believers. As the historian Eusebio Leal commented, "I would prefer a Christian revolutionary fighting at my side, defending this land palm by palm, to a false communist." The possibility of being elected to the National Assembly was also opened up for Christians, and at the next general election, two pastors, Raúl Suárez (see box) and Sergio Arce, were elected.

From the Cane Fields to International Ministry

Raúl Suárez Ramos was born in 1935 into a poor family in Aguacate, Havana Province. During the four-month sugar cane season, his father cut cane while Raúl's mother and ten children did odd jobs—washing clothes, running errands—to help make ends meet. During the eight-month dead season, the whole family would head for the mountains to make charcoal. Raúl was the only one in the family who learned to read. After reading the Gospels he decided to become a Christian.

Raúl left home at eighteen, and after a time of despair he had a deep faith experience that changed his life. He asked God to lead him into socially useful work. A Baptist pastor helped him cover eight grades of school in a year and a half, after which he entered the Baptist Seminary in Havana in 1955. He finished seminary and high school in the same year and then studied philosophy and letters at the University of Havana for a year in 1960. By that time, he was losing contact with his peasant origins and moving into the middle class.

Invited to serve a church in Havana, Raúl heard a voice calling him to work among the poor, so he went to a very poor church in Ciénega de Zapata. Living and working with the charcoal workers of the Zapata swamp became a second conversion experience for him. During this period, he married Clara Rodés, a Baptist lay pastor.

At the time of the Bay of Pigs invasion in 1961, the swamp area was attacked by mercenary parachutists, and Raúl was recruited as a Red Cross driver to take wounded Cubans to the hospital—an unforgettable experience that filled him with strong patriotic feelings. He was injured in one eye by nearby bazooka explosions.

Influenced by the anticommunism of U.S. missionaries, Raúl found it difficult to accept Castro's declaration of socialism. But his extraordinary

Rev. Raúl Suárez, pastor of Ebenezer Baptist Church, former president of the Cuban Ecumenical Council, and member of the National Assembly, leads a Bible study group.

sympathy for Fidel and Raúl Castro, Camilo Cienfuegos, and other revolutionary leaders, his loyalty to his origins, and the transformations he saw around him led him to become a supporter of the revolution. He began to see how one could live the gospel in a revolutionary situation and how Marxist criticism could help to deepen the authenticity of Christian faith. His encounter with Marxism stimulated him to find a new understanding of the Bible, liturgy, and Cuban history.

In 1971 Raúl, Clara, and their three children moved to Marianao, a working-class section in Havana, where Raúl became pastor of Ebenezer Baptist Church. Under his leadership the church developed a strong program of Bible study, community service, ecumenical relationships, and lay leadership. In 1977 Raúl received a theological degree from the Baptist Seminary in Mexico City and in 1980 a license in history from the University of Havana. That year he also began teaching history at Matanzas Seminary. As executive secretary of the Cuban Ecumenical Council from 1983 to 1987, he founded a commission responsible for ecological, agricultural, and humanitarian projects.

In 1987 Ebenezer Church inaugurated the Dr. Martin Luther King, Jr., Memorial Center, an ecumenical organization that works with the Cuban people in five major areas: theological and biblical studies, popular grass-roots education, integral service to the community, promotion of international solidarity, and communications. The church has two partner churches, one in Richmond, Virginia, and one in Carbondale, Illinois.

As president of the Cuban Ecumenical Council (1987–1991), Raúl was responsible for two important meetings between Evangelical church leaders and Castro that opened up new space for the church in Cuba. On Christmas Day 1990 an ecumenical service was broadcast from Ebenezer—the first religious broadcast in nearly thirty years. In January 1992 Clara Rodés having completed her seminary education and a long struggle to be accepted for ordination, became one of the first Baptist women to be ordained, becoming co-pastor of Ebenezer Church. In need of a kidney transplant, and medicine unavailable because of the blockade, she died during an operation in 1994.

Raúl was elected to the National Assembly of Cuba in 1993 and reelected in 1998. He serves on the Foreign Policy Committee. The three children—an electrical engineer, a doctor, and a cinema and television professional—take active leadership roles in the church and the King Center.

In many ways, the story of Raúl's life from his poor origins in the cane fields of Aguacate to his multifaceted national and international ministry based in Marianao is the story of Cuba itself and how that small island, despite heartaches and hurdles, has an important role to play on the world stage.

〰〰〰〰〰〰〰〰〰〰〰〰〰〰〰〰

Rectification and Special Period

In 1986 Cuba came to a moment of crisis. Domestic problems were growing. Personal corruption and economic mismanagement were rampant. Economic incentives were crowding out moral incentives. Cuba was relying too much on foreign (Soviet) models. Castro described the situation:

> The Party was starting to go to pot. . . . When mistakes are not energetically fought, the people start to become skeptical, discouraged, and demoralized; the revolution's ideals are discredited. . . . The construction of socialism is essentially a political task, a revolutionary task. It must be educating people. . . . This doesn't deny the usefulness and necessity of economic mechanisms. But to me it's clear that economics is an instrument of political and revolutionary work. (*Granma Weekly Review*, Dec.14, 1986)

The name given to this process of analyzing the problems and taking corrective action was "rectification"—rectifying the mistakes and errors of the past. As Juan Antonio Blanco, founder and director of the Felix Varela Center in Havana, put it,

> We realized that we could not develop an alternative society based on solidarity and feelings of love for your neighbor while using capitalist economic incentives, which foster a dog-eat-dog mentality. So we recaptured the use of moral incentives, which had been set aside for nearly 15 years. We did not discard material incentives, we understood that material incentives were also important to motivate people. But little by little we began to recover the idea that the revolution was not only a matter of a more just distribution of wealth, but also a spiritual project to release people's creativity and give them a greater degree of participation in society. (Blanco and Benjamin, *Cuba*, p. 28)

Rectification has brought a new vitality and energy to the revolution at all levels and in all areas. And it has brought a new appreciation for the legacy of Che Guevara, who was a strong proponent of moral incentives and an outspoken critic of what he saw to be an authoritarian and bureaucratic European socialism.

In 1990–1991 Cuba came to another crisis moment, perhaps the greatest one of all: the collapse of the Soviet bloc. When the United States cut off trade with Cuba, the Soviet Union had come to the rescue of Cuba as a trading partner and saved it from demise. The Soviet collapse of 1989 changed everything. As Marc Frank commented in *Cuba Looks to the Year 2000* (1993),

> Cuba's entire economy rested on the following assumptions: stable and expanding markets for Cuban sugar and other exports; stable and expanding supplies of oil and other strategic materials; trade through barter and rubles, and not hard currency; preferential trade terms and development credits to help Cuba overcome the legacy of Spanish colonialism and U.S. neocolonialism; and five-year agreements that allowed Cuba to make long-term development plans. . . . (p.141)

> Such a dramatic drop of close to 100% of Cuban foreign aid and well over 50% of its traditional trade, plus the loss of membership in a large market that is a must for a small country like Cuba, would be enough to devastate any nation. But there was more: virtually all of Cuba's industry and machinery came from the former European socialist countries. Most of Cuba's plants were built to their specifications, relying on materials and spare parts available only in a socialist Europe that had disappeared, and often from companies that had closed up shop. Finally, Cuba faced increasing U.S. efforts to block any attempt to secure aid, trade, markets, materials, and parts from new sources. (p.144)

Calling this new development the Special Period in Peacetime, the government took drastic steps to restructure its economy, reduce consumption, save energy, cope with rising unemployment and scarcity, and devise alternative ways of "making do." As bus transportation stopped, people started riding bicycles. Farmers went back to plowing with oxen. Street lighting and air conditioning were reduced, evening events were canceled, newspapers and television broadcasting were decreased, and people without jobs were helped to find other work in the same province and given the same salaries as before. An interesting comment on the Special Period came from blacks: they were already used to it; they (all through earlier Cuban history) had always been living in a "special period," and now the special period was for all.

Why did the Soviet Union fall? The conventional answer in the West is that the collapse of the socialist economy was propelled by the inherent weakness in socialism and in a centrally planned economy. But David Kotz and Fred Weir point out in "Why Did the USSR Fall? The Party Elite, Not the Masses, Wanted Capitalism" in *Dollars and Sense* (July/August 1997):

> In contrast to the conventional wisdom, the Soviet revolution of 1991 was made, not against the small elite that ran the Soviet Union, but rather by that elite. And it was not collapse of the USSR's planned economy that drove this process, because no such collapse took place. . . . The Soviet elite dismantled their own system in pursuit of personal enrichment. Correctly understood, the USSR's downfall was caused by the undemocratic features of its system, not by the failure of economic planning.

This interpretation gives more importance to Cuba's rectification process, which perceived the dangers in the Soviet model and made corrections in the Cuban model to make it more Cuban.

CONTINUED U.S. HOSTILITY

In early 1962 the United States extended its embargo on U.S.-Cuban trade to a blockade that included all ships, from any country, that contained Cuban products. The blockade was both the constricting context for, and a destabilizing counterforce to, Cuba's new era of self-management.

Operation Mongoose, described earlier, continued into 1962. When Cuba learned that U.S. General Edward Lansdale, coordinator of Operation Mongoose, was planning an invasion for October, it accepted the offer of the Soviet Union (which wanted a base near the United States) to send intermediate-range nuclear missiles for the defense of the island. When the United States discovered Soviet missiles in Cuba and learned more were on the way in Soviet freighters, it immediately instituted a U.S. naval blockade of Cuba and threatened a nuclear confrontation with the Soviet Union. Through a series of letters, President Kennedy and Premier

Nikita Khrushchev reached an settlement that averted war: the Soviet Union agreed to withdraw its missiles from Cuba, and the United States agreed to end the naval blockade (though not the commercial blockade) and pledged not to invade Cuba.

Operation Mongoose was disbanded, but Task Force W, the CIA unit in that operation, continued its covert activities of raids, sabotage, and bombings through the use of Cuban exile groups and agents. When Richard Nixon became president in January 1969, he directed the CIA to increase its covert actions against Cuba.

Cuba began to suffer a series of epidemics that suggested bacteriological warfare. In May 1971 African swine fever appeared in Cuba—the first time in the Western Hemisphere. (The U.S. press reported several years later that an intelligence source had confessed transferring swine fever germs from Fort Gulich in Panama to Miami-based Cuban contras just before the epidemic broke out.) Tobacco's blue mold and a number of other plagues struck the island's key crops and livestock in the 1970s and early 1980s. In 1981, 344,230 Cubans were hit by a hemorrhagic dengue epidemic. Dengue, carried by mosquitoes, appeared on the same day at both ends of the island—its first appearance in Cuba. The United States blocked Cuba's first efforts to purchase fumigators and chemicals to keep it from spreading. Many people suffered liver damage, and 158 people died. Eduardo Arocena, on trial for drug trafficking in 1981, testified that he had personally transferred dengue germs to Cuba in 1980. In the late 1970s and early 1980s, there were also five separate outbreaks of hemorrhagic conjunctivitis (Franklin, "War Against Cuba," *Covert Action Quarterly*, 1998, pp. 31–32; Frank, *Cuba Looks*, pp. 160–62).

PROTECTING THE GAINS OF THE REVOLUTION: ANOTHER TIME OF TRANSITION (1991–)

Struggling under the massive blows of the demise of Soviet bloc support and intensification of the U.S. blockade (see below), Cuba sought to introduce enough market mechanisms to enable its survival without giving up the valued gains of the revolution. As Castro commented, "We are walking over broken glass and at times we don't know where to put our feet."

Modification in the Economy

Needing hard currency to buy goods in the world market and to pay for its social programs, in 1992 Cuba introduced U.S. currency as official tender (along with the Cuban peso). The government established joint ventures with foreign corporations (especially to build tourist hotels), opened stores and markets that accepted only dollars, and encouraged the tourist industry (for non-U.S. visitors)—all measures that brought in hard currency. The government allowed Cubans to sell their garden crops, after meeting state quotas, in free markets and to operate small restaurants (using only family members) in their homes. These enterprises were heavily taxed. Through all these liberalizing changes, however, certain basic principles were not negotiable; the ownership of land and the means of production were to remain in the hands of the Cuban government.

To earn hard currency, Castro has encouraged joint ventures with the government and foreign corporations to build luxurious tourist hotels.

Along with the benefits of modification came significant debits. The new economic approaches brought a two-tiered economy—those who had dollars (perhaps half the population) and those who had only pesos from their government salaries. During the era of Soviet subsidy, when prices were low, salaries were adequate, but they have been frozen for ten years while prices have risen sharply, except for such government-subsidized basics as rice and dried beans (*New York Times*, January 11, 1999).

Blanco, in *Cuba: Talking About Revolution*, discusses both the upside and downside of tourism: its bringing in hard currency to maintain the nation's access to the most basic necessities of life—food, health care, education—but also its development of "tourist apartheid" (hotels available only to foreigners) and prostitution.

In general, I see the development of the tourist industry at this time as a kind of chemotherapy for the economy. When you have a cancer, sometimes the only option that you have available is to go through chemotherapy. And as we know, chemotherapy has such terrible side effects that it can even kill you before you die from the cancer.

Well, the Cuban economy at this moment has a cancer, and we have to take radical decisions in order to keep it afloat. We need to keep the economy afloat because we want to maintain the free educational system, the health care system, food security, the social security system. And to keep all that running, you need to get as much hard currency as possible, in the shortest possible time. (p. 42)

Vitality of Church Life

Today the churches show great vitality. Most Evangelical churches are full on Sunday mornings, with many new members joining. Many churches have community outreach programs, conducting workshops on different subjects, operating a hotline staffed by a psychologist member, working with prostitutes, opening their church libraries to the neighborhood. Four in Havana have adjacent dormitories to house visitors and people who come for conferences and workshops.

The Martin Luther King, Jr., Memorial Center in Havana, established by Ebenezer Baptist Church in 1987, operates a conference center and dormitory and carries on a vital local, national, and international ministry offering lay educational programs, theological institutes, neighborhood housing renovation, and communications and publications outreach. It serves as the national reception point for all Pastors for Peace caravans and shipments of medical supplies. The center has become known all over Cuba.

The Council of Churches of Cuba now has twenty-one member churches (including Methodist, Presbyterian, Episcopal, Baptist, Evangelical Lutheran, Church of God, Salvation Army, Friends, Christian Reformed, and Pentecostal). It has four observer churches, five ecumenical movements, six organizations with local group ties, and two fraternal members. The council in 1998 was sponsoring thirty-two projects in sustainable development (biogas, worm culture, renewable energy, potable water, organic agriculture, sustainable nutrition, and green medicine), eleven humanitarian aid projects (medicines), and ten ecumenical and social infrastructure projects (equipment for special schools, infant day-care centers, a psychiatric hospital, homes for the elderly, and renovation of houses in the barrios).

An historic event was the five-day visit of Pope John Paul II in January 1998. Castro, who had visited the pope in the Vatican in 1996 bearing an invitation, warmly welcomed his guest and urged Cubans to attend the outdoor masses in Santa Clara, Camagüey, Santiago de Cuba, and Havana. In addition, there were cordial meetings with both government leaders and Evangelical church leaders. The pope covered a number of subjects in his homilies—speaking out against abortion, divorce, premarital sex, boarding schools, the denial of human rights, the incarceration of "prisoners of conscience," the U.S. blockade, the seductive force of materialism, and the blind and dehumanizing market forces of global capitalism. He also argued for more space in Cuban society for the Roman Catholic Church—permitting it to open religious schools, use mass media channels, distribute church publications more widely, organize religion-based social groups, and receive more priests, seminarians, and nuns from abroad. Not mentioned was the fact that many Catholic schools before 1959 had been boarding schools and, even more seriously, centers for inculcating class, race, and gender divisions and inequities and counter-revolutionary consciousness. Whether the government could now recognize a sufficient "sea change" to consider granting such space was problematic.

In June 1998 Castro invited a delegation from the National Council of Churches to dinner and conversation in the palace. An account of that meeting forms the foreword of this book. In November the government gave permission to celebrate Christmas as a public holiday.

THE U.S. PERSPECTIVE AND FOREIGN REACTION

The United States continues to look upon Cuba as a country that needs to be brought around to the U.S. way of thinking and acting. Beginning in 1992, the United States took measures to tighten the thirty-year-old blockade:

The Torricelli Act

On October 24, 1992, President George Bush signed the Cuban Democracy Act (Torricelli Act), heavily influenced by Mas Canosa, head of the Cuban American National Foundation, and sponsored by Congressman Robert Torricelli of New Jersey. The act banned trade with Cuba by U.S. subsidiary companies based abroad, although, according to a Johns Hopkins University survey, 70 percent of recent sales was in food and medicine. It permitted the seizure and sale of any ship that docks in a U.S. port within six months after docking in Cuba. It reduced U.S. aid to any nation that imports Cuban sugar by the same dollar amount as the value of the sugar imported. It authorized the National Endowment for Democracy (NED) to fund Cuban "dissident" groups and directed the president to pressure countries to halt their trade with Cuba (Great Britain, France, Canada, Mexico, Japan). The act's stated purpose was "to promote a peaceful transition to democracy in Cuba through the application of appropriate pressures on the Cuban Government and support for the Cuban people." With the "stick" were several "carrots": the release of medical supplies currently denied; the easing of travel restrictions, allowing educational, cultural, and scientific exchanges; and restoration of direct phone and mail service. Normal bilateral relations would not be established, however, until a post-Castro administration established U.S.-style democratic institutions, reduced the Cuban armed forces, ended Cuban support for revolution abroad, and implemented a market economy.

Nations around the world opposed the extraterritorial measures in the act as against international law. Canada reminded U.S. subsidiaries in Canada of a 1984 law that any representative of a U.S. subsidiary that follows U.S. extraterritorial measures concerning trade with Cuba could face a fine of up to $10,000 or five years in jail, or both. Mexico stated that it would apply the severest measures against any national or foreign countries based in Mexico that observed the terms of the Torricelli Act.

On November 19, 1994, a Cuban exile organization, Brothers to the Rescue (founded in 1991 by Mas Canosa and veterans of the Bay of Pigs Brigade 2506 and Alpha 66, another CIA-supported operation) began penetrating Cuban air space, dropping leaflets over Cuban cities, urging the people to revolt. It also made plans for sabotage, commando raids, and assassination. After repeated complaints and warnings to the United States, the Cuban government took action on February 24, 1996, by shooting down two of the Brothers to the Rescue planes. The United States denounced the shooting, demanded compensation, and used the incident to gain support for the Helms-Burton Bill.

The Helms-Burton Act

On March 12, 1996, President Bill Clinton signed the Cuban Liberty and Domestic Solidarity Act (Helms-Burton Act). Designed to tighten the U.S. blockade of Cuba still further and press foreign investors to pull out of Cuba, it has also had the serious result of taking U.S. foreign policy toward Cuba out of the hands of the president and placing it under the control of Congress.

Two sections of the law have come under special condemnation from other countries: Title III (currently being postponed in six-month intervals) allows U.S. citizens and corporations to sue in U.S. courts foreign companies that "traffic" in property confiscated by the Cuban people in the 1960s. The total amount of these certified claims is $1.8 billion (not including interest). In addition, thousands of Cuban immigrants who are U.S. citizens today will be able to pursue "uncertified" claims in U.S. courts to try to get back their properties. According to U.S. lawyer Michael Krinsky, the United States' real demand is not compensation for property but its return; the aim is restore the old prerevolutionary wealthy class to its former position.

Title IV (already in effect) states that any company that commits further "trafficking" in confiscated property in Cuba after March 12, 1996, is subject to a U.S. travel ban. Already officers and family members of the Sherritt International Corporation of Canada (which has been operating a nickel mine jointly with a Cuban state-owned mining company for the last two years) and of the Mexican company Grupos Domos (which bought half of the Cuban telephone company in 1994) have been barred from entering the United States.

The Canadian attorney general has called the Helms-Burton Act a violation of international law and declared its extraterritorial reach unenforceable in Canada. Any Canadian corporation or individual who complies with it may be punished with stiff fines or imprisonment or both. To protest the absurdity of the U.S. laws, several members of Parliament have introduced bills seeking restitution of property taken from Canadians without compensation during the American Revolution in what is now Virginia, Pennsylvania, New York, and Massachusetts.

A coalition of twenty Canadian church and development organizations has made plans to launch a boycott of tourism in Florida if Title III is implemented. Nearly 2 million Canadians visit Florida every year, spending US$1.3 billion annually. "The U.S. government is using its economic might and political power to injure Cuban people and limit the freedom of the Canadian people," the coalition announced. "We are especially concerned because the Helms-Burton Law will harm the efforts of the Canadian church and aid organizations trying to help Cuba's poor." Members of the coalition include the Division of World Outreach of The United Church of Canada, the Canadian Catholic Organization for Development and Peace, OXFAM Canada, and seventeen other groups.

The opposition of other nations to the blockade has also been reflected in the United Nations. In 1998, for the seventh year in a row, the UN General Assembly voted overwhelmingly to end the U.S. economic embargo of Cuba. In 1992 the record was 59 to 3, with 71 abstentions, 46 not voting. In 1998 it was 157 to 2, with 12 abstentions. The only nation that joined the United States in voting against the Cuban resolution in 1998 was Israel.

Sabotage

Meanwhile, sabotage efforts have continued. On October 21, 1996, a U.S. State Department S2R fumigation plane flying along the international air corridor over Matanzas Province was observed discharging a liquid over the crops below. Soon after, the Thrips palmi insect plague, which causes severe damage to maize, bean, squash, cucumber, and other food crops, appeared in the fields below the corridor—a disease that was previously unknown in Cuba. Since then the plague has affected some nine thousand hectares of seventeen different agricultural crops (Franklin, "War Against Cuba," p.33; Diaz, "New Biological Attacks by the United States," *Granma International*, May 27, 1997, p. 4).

In the summer of 1997 a bombing campaign against tourist hotels in Havana, masterminded by a Cuban exile terrorist, Luis Posada Carriles (trained by the CIA and funded by the Cuban American National Foundation), was carried out by a Salvadoran mercenary.

In October 1997 another attempt was made to assassinate Fidel Castro. Four men with CIA and CANF connections, carrying sophisticated assassination equipment, headed from Miami to Venezuela's Margarita Island, where Castro was going to address a meeting. When the boat encountered engine problems, it drew the attention of the U.S. Coast Guard, which discovered the concealed arms and intention of the trip and arrested the men (Franklin, "War Against Cuba," pp. 30–31).

One further episode of destabilization needs to be mentioned—a very significant one, for it lays out the basic objectives of the United States. On February 3, 1997, the Clinton administration, in compliance with the Helms-Burton Act, released a twenty-four-page report, "Support for a Democratic Transition in Cuba," that spells out the administration's plan for a post-Castro "democratization" and economic "liberalization" program. It calls for the downsizing and privatization of the Cuban health and education systems; a restructuring and privatization of the banks, industries, state enterprises, public services, and utilities; a reform of the tax, budgetary, legal, and legislative systems; the restoration of all properties to the pre-1959 owners; the installation of the long-term U.S. advisers; and an economy under the discipline of the International Monetary Fund and World Bank. In effect, this plan would restore Cuba to its pre-1959 status as a U.S. colony. In exchange, for the six years following the establishment of transition government, Cuba would receive from $4 billion to $8 billion in loans, donations, and guarantees from outside sources, a bargain price for gaining control of Cuba's assets once again.

A CUBAN PERSPECTIVE

Cubans are a strong, resilient, resourceful, innovative people. Their ability to survive, despite the hostility of their nearest neighbor to the north, proves this. Their nation is going through another time of testing, another period of coping and transition. It is not clear what the future will hold.

For Cuba to be able to save its independence, social justice and ethic of solidarity—more than even before—it will have to be Martí's Republic "with all for the good of all."

It will not be a proliferation of political parties but the broadest possible pluralism that will unleash our collective and creative imagination.

It is not the privatization but the socialization of the management of state property, today administered bureaucratically, which can restore our faith in the future.

It is not the anarchic destabilization of our reality but its gradual—and timely—transformation, which can assure the possibility of our future victory.

It is not the financial or bureaucratic manipulation of civil society but its still greater autonomous and participatory activity and decision making from which a new and democratic culture will emerge.

It is not the free market and representative democracy but democratic planning and participatory political democracy—within the solid framework of a lawful state—which can ensure the operation and full enjoyment for everyone of their political, civil, economic, social and cultural rights.

It will not be the philosophy of consumerism but that of the equality of life which will make possible an ecologically sustainable and socially responsible human development.

It is not the ethic of "having" but the ethic of "being" which today can lead us out of the labyrinth in which not only Cuba, but all of humanity finds itself.

This is why Cuba's destiny is relevant to the rest of the world. (Blanco and Benjamin, *Cuba: Talking About Revolution*, p.132–133)

Questions for Reflection

1. Today more blacks own their homes in Cuba than in any other country (Casal, in *The Cuba Reader*, Brenner, p. 482). In the United States how can barriers limiting the access of blacks to home ownership and employment be eliminated?
2. Cuba has made great efforts to make education available to everyone. U.S. public education is open to all but it varies greatly in quality depending on the location. What could be done to equalize educational opportunities? Where would funds come from?
3. Cuba has done much to elevate the position of women but machismo remains a problem. Is it a problem in the United States and Canada? What might be done about it?
4. If Cuba, a poor country, can provide free health care to all its citizens plus many visitors, why cannot richer nations do so too? What is the effect of the profit motive on health care?
5. What does the contrast between the low funding given to the arts in public schools and the National Endowment for the Arts and the high salaries paid to a few sports and entertainment figures say about U.S. values.
6. Cuba, which has virtually no private enterprise, has no high salaries and few homeless. In the United States, the average compensation for chief executive officers is 209 times higher than that of factory workers, and there are lots of jobless and lots of homeless. What could Cuba teach us to help solve these problems?

7. Considering all that Cuban block organizations (CDRs) do to improve life in their communities, what would you think of national programs to develop block organizations across the United States and Canada to bring people closer together? What could such local groups do?

8. Because it costs a lot of money to run for office in the United States, a successful candidate has to spend a lot of time and effort in fundraising and often seems to pay more attention to the people who contributed to his campaign than to the people he is supposed to represent. What merit do you see in the Cuban election system? Why should Cubans be pressed to adopt the U.S. system?

9. Are individual rights or collective rights more important in Cuba? In the United States? In Canada?

10. Fidel Castro said that religion can be an opiate or a wonderful cure depending on how it is used. Do you agree? What examples can you see in Cuba and in your own country?

CHAPTER 4
CUBAN ÉMIGRÉS

Migration is a Cuban fact of life. During Cuba's early history, as described in the previous chapters, most migration was into Cuba. Since the late nineteenth century, there has been much migration out of Cuba. Existing so close to the highly developed metropolitan center that is the United States has had a profound effect upon Cuba. Not only has that center influenced Cuba's culture, it has also exerted a strong gravitational pull on Cuba's population.

During the last third of the nineteenth century, some hundred thousand Cubans emigrated to the United States, as well as to Europe and the more developed parts of Latin America. Substantial Cuban communities developed in Key West and Tampa (where Cubans worked in cigar factories) and in Miami, Union City, New Jersey, and New York City. In the twentieth century northward migration from less developed countries in the south (not only from Cuba but also from Mexico, Puerto Rico, Haiti, and others) to the highly developed metropolitan center greatly increased. A study made by the Kettering Foundation in the early 1970s found that one out of every three persons in Latin America wanted to migrate to the United States. If this projection were applied to Cuba, it would suggest a potential 4 million-person exodus from the island—a figure far beyond what has taken place so far.

As Jesús Arboleya points out in his book *Havana-Miami: The U.S.-Cuba Migration Conflict* (1996),"The act of emigrating is generally a complex, traumatic decision which has many causes, and it reflects to some extent the individual's dissatisfaction with their [sic] situation or with what they [sic] expect to get out of life. In such a framework it is nearly impossible to discern where economic influence ends and where the political—or even psychological—one begins" (p.10).

In the case of Cubans, this complexity of motivation can include such factors as disagreement with political, social, and economic directions of the revolution; disappointment in career advancement or remuneration; desire for family reunification; lack of access to dollars; frustration and suffering caused by the lack of consumer goods, transportation, housing, medicines, and other basic necessities (resulting primarily from the blocade and the collapse of the Soviet bloc); and general fatigue from the constant effort to cope.

POST-REVOLUTIONARY MIGRATIONS

Beyond this complexity of individual factors, however, is the larger geopolitical context. After 1959 the migratory process between Cuba and the United States became highly politicized. The exodus had important propaganda value for the United States, which saw it as proof of the lack of popular support for the Cuban revolution and the Castro government and evidence that there was political persecution in Cuba. Early émigrés were automatically accepted as political refugees. The United States also saw the exodus as having important strategic value. It was contributing to the brain drain of Cuban leaders and technical workers needed by the revolution. At the same time it was building a support base and personnel pool in the United States for counterrevolutionary efforts.

Thus the blockade, as a vise continually tightening on Cuba and as a generator of refugees, became an integral part of the United States' "low-intensity" war on Cuba. ("Low-intensity" is the U.S. term for unrelenting economic and psychological warfare. Cuba experiences this type of war as a "high-intensity" one in terms of its impact and basic goal.)

Post-revolutionary emigration occurred in four waves.

First Wave (1959–1962)

The first wave of emigration (between 1959 and 1962), was set off by the nationalization of agricultural properties, businesses, and schools and the confiscation of second homes. Some 125,000 Batista supporters, wealthy property owners, and upper-class business people and professionals affected by the nationalization left the country (see box).

An Émigré Bishop

Onell Soto was born in 1932 in Omaja, a small town founded by U.S. immigrants from Nebraska in Oriente Province. In 1938 his family moved to San Agustín, where his father was head of an army post. Onell attended Methodist primary and secondary schools in Omaja and

Matanzas on scholarship. He entered the University of Havana's School of Medicine in 1952, completing four years of study before the university was closed for political reasons. In 1956 he attended a World Student Christian Federation conference in Germany, which greatly broadened his vision.

In 1957 Onell went to the United States to study at Boston University. In January 1959 when his father was brought to trial as an army officer of the ousted regime, he returned to Cuba. A short trial in Victoria las Tunas condemned his father to death, but Onell prevailed upon the revolutionary authorities to grant a more formal trial, which took place later that month in Holguín. Just before the trial, Onell met the young captain in charge of his father. The captain told Onell, "You will hate me, because if your father is found guilty, we will have to execute him." "I will not hate you sir," Onell answered. "Are you a Christian?" the captain asked. "We are trying to be," Onell answered. "In the mountains American missionaries taught me the Christian faith," the captain said, and Onell could see his body language change.

After a nearly three-hour evening trial, the five judges gave Onell's father a thirty-year sentence. The captain then came to Onell and his sister and said, "Let us go and see the old man." So they went to the prison where his father was. It was already 11:00 P.M. When the prisoner heard the approaching footsteps, he thought the end had come. Instead, he was able to embrace his son. The captain then said, "Why don't we have a moment of prayer?" and asked Onell to pray.

The elder Soto was imprisoned first on the Isle of Pines, and later transferred to prisons in Santiago de Cuba and Holguín. Finally after thirteen years, he was released. He worked for a time as a barber in Omaja, and then emigrated to the United States in 1979.

Meanwhile, Onell Soto worked for two years as a chemical technician at a flour mill in Havana and helped support his mother. In July 1960 he married Nina Ulloa, director of Christian education for the Episcopal Church in Cuba, and became an Episcopalian. Later that year the couple moved to the United States for a short visit but decided to stay.

In 1964 Soto received an STM from the School of Theology of the University of the South at Sewanee, Tennessee (which later granted him a DD). After further studies at the Episcopal Seminary of the Southwest in Austin, Texas, he began an international ministry, serving as vicar in Quito, Ecuador, executive secretary of Province IX (covering Mexico, Central America, Ecuador, Colombia, Dominican Republic, and Puerto Rico), mission education officer at the Episcopal headquarters in New York, and bishop of Venezuela. He is now assistant bishop of Atlanta. He has four children and three grandchildren. Bishop Soto is one of ten Cuban-born

Episcopalian bishops who have served in Latin America and the United States. He guesses that the reason there are so many bishops from Cuba might be because of Cubans' capacity for hard work, perseverance, and willingness to serve anywhere in the world. Also their native Spanish language is a benefit to mission work.

~~~ ~~~ ~~~ ~~~ ~~~ ~~~ ~~~ ~~~ ~~~ ~~~ ~~~ ~~~ ~~~ ~~~ ~~~

They came primarily to Miami but also to the Union City area and to New York City. Most expected to stay only a few years before the revolution would be reversed and they could return to their former positions and properties. (Many lost this hope, however, after the Bay of Pigs defeat and the missile crisis agreement between the United States and Cuba.) Because of the leading roles these first émigrés had played in trade, investment, and management in pre-revolutionary Cuba, they were quickly integrated into the U.S. business world, helping to make Miami the financial center for all of Latin America. Miami had many similarities to Batista's Havana—the same class distinctions and racial biases, as well as gambling, prostitution, sweat shops, and a thriving drug trade.

In 1961, when the revolution was declared socialist, a large number of religious people began leaving for the United States. As Margaret E. Crahan has written,

At the outset of the Cuban Revolution most church people expected the government to implement substantial, but not radical, change. While there had been fairly widespread support on the part of the churches for the overthrow of the Batista dictatorship, there was little expectation of substantial land reform, nationalization of foreign holdings, or the emergence of a single-party Communist state.

The Catholic and Protestant churches, together with the Jewish community, were largely unprepared to respond positively to such changes as they lacked organizational flexibility, ideological and political openness, and commitment to substantial socioeconomic change.

All were closely linked to foreign institutions as sources of funding and personnel. Approximately 2,500 out of 3,000 Catholic priests and religious in Cuba in 1959 were from Spain, while the principal Protestant denominations were U.S.-based missionary operations. . . . Such ties encouraged Cuban church people to leave, and by 1965, 20% of Catholic priests and 90% of religious . . . had done so, while over 50% of Protestant clerical and lay leaders departed. ("Freedom of Worship in Revolution Cuba," in *The Cuba Reader*, Brenner)

As with the earlier secular migration, these religious émigrés were primarily from the upper and middle class (see box). In contrast, clergy and lay people who came from peasant and worker backgrounds saw the revolution in a much different light, most of them opting to remain.

~~~~~~

A New Life in a New Land

Manuel Fernandez was born in Cuba to the parents of Spanish immigrants from Asturias. His father worked as a bartender, his mother as a domestic until they had saved enough to buy a bar-grocery in 1934. Both parents worked sixteen hours a day seven days a week to establish themselves in Cuba's large middle class. They sent both Manuel and his sister to private Catholic schools and belonged to a Spanish organization that provided health insurance at reasonable rates. Manuel went on to La Salle College and in 1959 got a job teaching business skills at his own secondary school, La Salle Academy.

When the revolutionary government took over the private schools in 1960 and forbade any mention of religion in the classrooms, Fernandez was given the choice to keep his job or to leave. Although he was not a political activist and had said nothing against Castro, he was considered "too much of a Catholic" at a time when religious affiliation was frowned on and often penalized. At his mother's urging, he went to stay with relatives in Spain. There he studied at the University of Madrid, but job prospects looked poor.

In January 1963, Fernandez arrived in New York with little money and less English. He went to work washing floors in the cafeteria at Briarcliff College and within two years was assistant manger of Saga Food Service, which ran the cafeteria. To avoid a transfer to Boston, he became a personal loan interviewer for First National City Bank, a job that used his Spanish.

In 1967 Fernandez went to Bishop Ford Diocesan High School in Brookly to teach Spanish. At the same time he coached track and then baseball. At night he went to Mercy College at Dobb's Ferry for a B.A. in bilingual education (1975) and to St. John's University in Queens for a certificate in administration (1985). For the last fifteen years he has been dean of students at Ford.

Meanwhile, Fernandez's parents' shop had been nationalized, and his father had become ill and in need of medicine not available in Cuba. In 1969 he brought his parents and sister to New York. They maintained a Cuban household, speaking Spanish and eating rice and beans, traditions that Fernandez and his niece, married to a Puerto Rican, continue. Fernandez allows that émigrés of an older generation still dream of returning to a restored, post-Castro Cuba, but he himself would only go back for a visit for old times' sake. He has no wish to return permanently to a country where people are not free to criticize the government or elect candidates without government approval. He has made a new life in the United States, without losing his Spanish tradition, and when he retires, he thinks of Mexico rather than Cuba.

≈≈≈≈≈≈≈≈≈≈≈≈≈≈≈

Later in 1961, the U.S. State Department, CIA, and Roman Catholic Church initiated Operation Peter Pan—a program disseminating antigovernment rumors (described in the last chapter) that caused panic among parents and resulted in the migration of fifteen thousand children to the United States. They were placed in camps and foster homes until their parents were able to join them several years later.

Direct flights between Cuba and the United States were ended by President Kennedy in 1962, forcing émigrés to travel by way of third countries. During this time the Cuban emigration policy remained the same: Cubans were free to leave Cuba legally if they had a visa from another country. U.S. immigration policy, however, was no longer a coherent one. Legal émigrés found it hard to get visas, but illegal émigrés were welcomed with open arms as political refugees: they were granted green cards, Social Security, Medicare, and a chance to apply for citizenship after a year of residency—all of which encouraged greater illegal emigration.

Second Wave (1965–1973)

In 1965 a second major migration wave started—first with a boatlift from Camarioca, and then with "freedom flights" from Varadero to Miami that transported 3,000 to 4,000 persons a month—268,000 in all. Most of these émigrés were also upper and middle class and well educated; 90 percent had relatives in the United States. All were granted political asylum. The airlift was ended by President Nixon in 1973.

Third Wave (1979–1984)

A significant new stage of emigration began in 1979. During that year approximately a hundred thousand Cuban-Americans from Miami came back to visit family members, bringing gifts worth thousands of dollars—symbols of the affluent life available in the United States. President Jimmy Carter also extended a general invitation to Cubans to emigrate, and the Voice of America frequently played a song ("Come over to America, come over and be a hero") on its radio programs beamed to Cuba.

These influences brought an increase in popular seizures of ships and planes, and the breaking into several Latin American embassies by individuals hoping to obtain visas for emigration to the United States through third countries. Early in 1980, twelve persons forced their way into the Peruvian embassy in Havana and were given asylum. Other individuals also sought to break in, killing a Cuban guard in the process. The Cuban government then withdrew this protection, and in less than seventy-two hours, there were ten thousand people crowded into the embassy grounds. News of these developments appeared widely in U.S. newspapers but not news of subsequent developments a week later: more than 1 million Cubans marched past the Peruvian embassy to demonstrate their support for the revolution, and 5 million more marched in various cities across the island.

Cuba finally announced that everyone who wanted to emigrate could do so without a visa, and it urged those occupying the embassy to return home and wait for boats to pick them up. The port of Mariel was then designated to receive boats from the United States.

There were a number of new factors influencing this third migration: the contrast between the abundance in the United States and the scarcity in Cuba; the belief that riches were easy to come by; frustration and fatigue from trying to cope with all the difficulties and shortages of everyday existence; and loss of hope for any immediate improvement.

The 125,000 immigrants who suddenly arrived in the United States in the Mariel boatlift of 1980 overwhelmed the capabilities of U.S. Naturalization and Immigration. There were also new rules: the émigrés, many of whom were "undesirables" let out of Cuban prisons, were not granted automatic political asylum or special social assistance but were placed at first in detention camps in the southern part of the United States for processing. Nor was this newest wave welcomed as warmly by the exile community. For the first time the exodus included a large number of blacks and mulattos. These found themselves relegated to a much lower level in the Miami social hierarchy and encountered discrimination in their search for employment, housing, and social assistance. Across the nation U.S. public support for Cuban emigration also began to change.

Out of this crisis a new Migration Accord was worked out in 1984. The United States agreed to accept up to 20,000 legal immigrants (plus 3,000 political prisoners) each year, and Cuba agreed to repatriate 2,746 "excludables"—émigrés who had a previous criminal record in Cuba or who had violated laws in the United States. Most of these incarcerated Cubans had been held in the Federal Penitentiary in Atlanta and in the maximum security prison in Marion, Illinois. When I was a pastor in Carbondale, Illinois, I served as a pastoral visitor at the Marion Penitentiary. One of the Cubans I visited monthly was a black man who believed in Santeria. On one visit he mentioned that he had been crying for several days because a guard had torn up his most prized possession, a picture of St. Lazarus.

Fourth Wave (1990–1994)

In 1990 the migration process approached another crisis. The United States was granting an average of only 2,500 visas per year out of the 20,000 that the 1984 accord allowed. Determined émigrés began to leave the island on rafts and in hijacked boats. Cuba then decided to remove all restrictions on illegal departures and allowed ships from other countries to pick up emigrants. Twenty-nine thousand émigrés set out for Florida in the summer of 1994.

Meanwhile mass demonstrations in opposition to the emigration and in support of the Cuban government were taking place in different parts of the island. One mass rally in Havana, called to protest the murder of a young police officer by hijackers trying to commandeer a local ferry to the United States, drew half a million people. The United States, fearing another Mariel experience, refused to admit the émigrés. Officials eventually placed 40,000 émigrés in wire-enclosed tent detention camps at Guantánamo and another 10,000 in camps in Panama. In the fall of 1994 more than 8,400 military personnel were managing the Guantánamo camps, trying to contain rising tensions that produced riots, lawsuits, violence, and sixty suicide attempts—a $250 million operation.

To break this impasse, the United States and Cuba in September 1994 agreed to a revised Migration Accord. The United States promised to accept a minimum of 20,000 émigrés a year, to grant visas to the 19,000 Cubans currently on the waiting list, and to begin returning émigrés without visas to Cuba. Cuba, in return, agreed to reinstate its policy of discouraging illegal emigration. In December 1994 the Clinton administration agreed to admit 7,500 Guantánamo detainees with special needs: parents with children, the elderly over seventy, and the sick. In May 1995, in a further agreement, the U.S. government would allow some 21,000 Cubans held at Guantánamo to enter the United States at a rate of 500 a month, to be credited against the 20,000 annual allotment of Cuban émigrés; Cuba would accept all Cubans who wanted to return or who were deemed ineligible for entry into the United States.

Cuba had hoped in all of these discussions with the United States to address what it considered to be the real cause of the migration—the economic blockade and the U.S. attempt to force the Cuban people to surrender as a result of stress, hunger, and disease. But the United States refused to include this broader subject in the discussions.

THE CUBAN EXILE COMMUNITY

The two chief centers of Cuban exiles, to use the term that many émigrés prefer, are southern Florida and New Jersey, two pivotal states where exiles have the power to swing a vote and therefore have great influence on Washington.

Florida

In 1960 the Hispanic population of Dade Country, Florida (which includes Miami), was only 5 percent. As successive waves of Cuban immigrants arrived in the 1960s, they became a dominant element. Little Havana, as their central area of Miami was called, became their cultural center. Calle Ocho (Eighth Street) was lined with Spanish-speaking stores, coffee bars, and restaurants. Máximo Gómez Park offered a place for continuous domino games. St. John Bosco Catholic Church was founded in 1963 to meet the spiritual and social needs of the exiles.

Many of these newcomers, already well educated and experienced in business and the professions, succeeded in making comfortable lives. One notable example is the Fanjul family, who had dominated the Cuban sugar industry before the revolution. Taking advantage of a U.S. government water-control project in the Everglades and their close relations with the Dominican government, they made huge profits on their U.S. and Dominican plantations (*Time*, Nov. 23, 1998). Headquartered in Palm Beach they gave money to the sugar lobby in Congress, which subsidizes U.S. sugar prices, and contributed funds to the Democratic presidential campaign of 1992.

In the 1980s, immigrants began flooding in from many countries. By 1995, Dade County's population was 56 percent Hispanic. Of these, about 60 percent were Cuban Americans. This new diversity was reflected in the parish of St. John Bosco, which is now 68 percent Nicaraguan. The continuing arrival of twenty thousand Cubans or more each year, however, will undoubtedly bring an increasing "Cubanization" to Miami.

In the early years after the triumph of the revolution, the Cubans remaining on the island had feelings of great bitterness toward those who immediately left for Miami, calling them *gusanos* (worms). An early Cuban film, *Los Sobresvivientes* (The Survivors) satirized the difficulties a wealthy family in the Miramar section of Havana had when all their servants had left and the family was forced to cope on its own.

The exile community in Miami felt just as bitter about individuals and organizations that they perceived to be supporters of Fidel Castro and communism. Speakers, artists, musicians, and representatives of organizations from Cuba or deemed sympathetic to Cuba were picketed, boy-

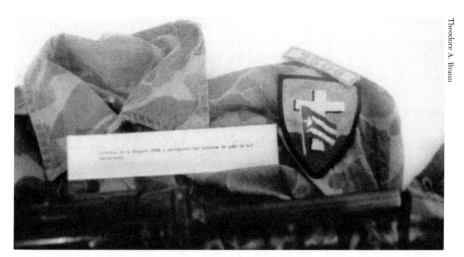

Uniform bearing insignia of the cross and Cuban flag was worn by an émigré who took part in the Bay of Pigs invasion in 1961.

cotted, threatened, and sometimes assassinated; and theaters, auditoriums, galleries, and radio stations hosting them were often threatened and sometimes bombed (Franklin, *Cuba and the United States*, pp. 87, 115, 121, 188, 200, 215, 268, 300). Tourist offices, airport facilities, and diplomatic missions of countries trading with Cuba were also bombed (Baker, *Cuba Handbook*, 1997, pp. 44, 45).

In addition, exiles variously took part in, organized, or supported armed efforts to eliminate Castro and overturn the revolution. Many of these efforts were encouraged and funded by the U.S. government, for example, an invasion from the Dominican Republic (1959) and the Bay of Pigs invasion (1961). Paramilitary exile groups such as Alpha 66, Omega 7, and Commanders of the United Revolutionary Organizations carried out terrorist activities in the United States.

Perhaps the most prominent Cuban exile in all these antirevolutionary efforts was Jorge Mas Canosa (see box). He also was a major figure, along with National Security Adviser Richard Allen, in creating in 1981 the Cuban American National Foundation (CANF), a key organization in the U.S. government's political and economic efforts to unseat Castro that remains part of the CIA's "program for public democracy."

〰〰〰〰〰〰〰〰〰〰〰〰〰〰〰
〰〰〰〰〰〰〰〰〰〰〰〰〰〰〰

A Determined Exile

During his lifetime, Jorge Mas Canosa (1939–1997) was one of the most powerful persons in the Cuban exile community in the United

States. Described as "imperious" and "unrelenting," he had a consuming passion to bring the Cuban revolution to an end and succeed Fidel Castro as president of a restored democratic Cuba.

Mas was born in Santiago de Cuba, the son of an army major. After a short time in college in North Carolina, he returned to Cuba in January 1959 and quickly became involved in anti-Castro student politics. Soon in trouble with the Castro government, he emigrated to the United States in 1960. There he joined the exile force being trained for the Bay of Pigs invasion, although he himself was sent in a diversionary unit to Santiago

Returning to the United States, he joined a CIA-sponsored training course in special missions and intelligence in Fort Benning, Georgia. Later, while doing blue-collar jobs in Miami, he continued to work with the anti-Castro movement. In 1971 he borrowed money to buy a small telephone services company, which did construction work for Southern Bell and eventually became the base of a telecommunications empire. At his death he was worth more than $100 million.

Mas became a U.S. citizen in 1980. The next year he was invited by the U.S. national security adviser to help create the Cuban American National Foundation (CANF) to direct and fund the anti-Castro struggle by influencing the U.S. government and public opinion. He also helped establish the National Endowment for Democracy, appointed by Congress, which gave the CANF more than $1 million in ten years.

Mas pushed through Congress such projects as Radio Martí (1982) and TV Martí(1990) to beam programs to Cuba. The TV programs, which reflect an anti-Castro point of view, have been jammed in Cuba. Mas also helped draft the Torricelli and Helms-Burton laws, intensifying the block-ade, and helped elect to Congress conservative members of the Cuban exile community in Florida (such as Ileana Ros-Lehtinen and Lincoln Díaz-Balart) and sympathetic candidates in other states (such as Robert Torricelli in New Jersey). He provided financial support for the covert operations of exile terrorists (such as Felix Rodriguez and Luis Posada) and exile groups such as Brothers to the Rescue (Franklin, *CovertAction*, Fall 1998; William Buckley, Jr., *National Review*, Dec. 31, 1997; James Wall, *Christian Century*, Sept. 7, 1994).

Some exiles felt that his pressure on Clinton to weaken Castro by stop-ping exiles sending aid to their families and reducing charter flights was doing more harm to Cubans than to Castro. Mas's death may make more space in the exile community for the voices of political moderates and a new generation of émigré leaders who are interested in reconciliation.

Time for Change

By Ninoska Perez Castellon

Editors' Note: The editors have included this article by the official spokesperson of the Cuban American National Foundation as another perspective on Cuba. The CANF is "the largest and by far the richest and most powerful of the exile groups [and] considers itself the Cuban government in exile" (Baker, Cuba Handbook, p.54). It claims that it supports the blockade in the hope of bringing down Castro and restoring democracy to Cuba. The article is an expression of CANF views. Many of its statements could be disputed. It does not represent the views of many other émigré groups.

Fidel Castro has been in power for forty years. The bearded rebel who captivated the world's imagination in 1959 has aged. The man who turned Cuba into a totalitarian state is now a septugenarian still dressed in fatigues and combat boots proclaiming an outdated slogan devoid of all options: "Socialism or death!" The dream of a revolution that would bring equality to the masses is nothing more than a bitter memory. Socialism is a slow death to which the Cuban people have been condemned.

In the name of a revolution one man sold Cuba's sovereignty to the Soviet Union for a huge subsidy. In the name of a revolution Cuban soldiers died fighting in international wars. In the name of a revolution Cubans live in a totalitarian state that has determined that a one-party rule has the right to deny them their basic freedoms.

As hard as it seems to understand, some still argue that Fidel Castro's permanency in power is justified, despite the fact that the Cuban people have not been able to cast their vote—freely and democratically—for the past four decades. If Castro is so popular and has such widespread support, why not hold elections? Why not allow political parties, other than the official Communist Party, to flourish? The last time I asked a Cuban official that question he responded by informing me that elections are held every five years. "Who ran against Castro in the last election?" was my next question. "That's not how we hold elections" was the curt reply. Obviously.

The sad part is that this type of response seems to be accepted by some who insist on changing Washington's policy toward Havana. With a degree of superiority over this Third World nation condemned to slavery, they will argue that it is a matter of cultures, as if Cubans were officially third class citizens. Are violations of human rights and lack of freedom deemed acceptable according to [a person's] race or geographic position?

Should the fact that thousands of men and women have suffered long sentences of twenty to thirty years in Castro's political prisons be considered a necessary evil? What has it achieved? Should it become an acceptable fact that they endured tortures, malnutrition, and the denial of medical care simply because they dissented? Should there be acceptance on our part even if it is still happening forty years later? Cuba presently has 241 prisons scattered throughout the island and it seems unlikely that the official sum of three hundred political prisoners would be the correct one. *[Amnesty International estimated three hundred to five hundred prisoners of conscience in 1992. Ed.]*

Granted that the Cuban Revolution has been tremendously successful in its propaganda, but it has been forty years of a totalitarian military dictatorship with one man at the helm. The documentary *This Is Cuba* shows a huge sign in a popular ice cream parlor in Havana: *"Aqui somos felices."* (We are happy here) despite the fact that those in line had been waiting for over four hours. Yes, we are happy here, but dissent is not tolerated and if you dare to raise your voice you end up in prison. Draconian terms such as *dangerousness* or *counterrevolutionary* will make sure of it. Yes we are happy here despite the fact that for years religion was banned in Cuba and atheism imposed on the population.

Now there are those who will argue that some change has taken place. *[There is now more tolerance of religion and a recognized Cuban Council of Churches, as discussed in chapter 3. Ed.]* Still, the regime determines the pace of change. Why? Would it be acceptable in the United States if the government controlled the churches or prohibited them from certain activities? Religious schools were banned by Fidel Castro in 1960 and have not been allowed since. In 1994 many Protestant groups started holding services in private homes. Soon thereafter Reverend Orson Vila was arrested as a signal that religious practices would not be tolerated if they could not be controlled by the state. The terms were laid down by Castro early on in the game: "Within the revolution, everything, outside, nothing."

To justify Fidel Castro's permanency in power, some will reason that education is free in Cuba. I like to think of this as the most widespread myth, because it never fails to amaze me how people can repeat this fallacy without analyzing its most basic aspects. So the government is going to teach your five-year-old to read and write? Well, to do so, it not only ties a red bandana around your child's neck but also imposes the communist ideology upon his mind. Would it be acceptable in the United States if to teach a child to read and write he had to belong to a specific political party? In this case, the only governing party? Would that classify as free education? What about the possibilities of furthering your career? For that, General Vecino Alegret, minister of Higher Education, has made it very clear in Cuba, *"The universities are for the revolutionaries."* Which of course leaves out all those who have dissented or whose families are not ardent supporters of the revolution. Certain books are banned, foreign newspapers are not allowed to circulate, antennas to monitor foreign TV stations are prohibited, and access to the Internet is unavailable. In a move some consider as a signal that change is taking place, CNN is allowed to have a news bureau in Cuba, but its information is strictly for consumption abroad and is not available to the Cubans in the island.

After the state has generously paid for your education, in the best tradition of servitude, you belong to the master. Once you become a professional you may not leave Cuba unless you are sent abroad—under contract—by the state, which will be paid by a foreign government for your services. Cuban professionals sent abroad may bring the state $60,000 a year, but the employee will be paid in Cuban pesos an equivalent of $100.00 a month. Foreign investors may rush to Cuba to build hotels or strip its mines, but Cubans are not allowed to participate in capitalist business ventures because that is a privilege reserved only for the government. To add insult to injury, Cubans are not allowed to stay in the luxurious hotels that cater only to foreigners with dollars. It's the same apartheid we criticized in South Africa, but some seem willing to accept Cuba's tropical version. The irony is that Cuban children according to the ration card are entitled to obtain milk—by paying for it, of course—only until they are seven years old. They blame this [restriction] on the economic embargo imposed by the United States. Yet tourists with dollars can have all the fresh milk they want in Cuba's new luxury hotels. Welcome to Cuba's version of equality.

Another widespread myth is Cuba's so-called excellent health-care system, which is supposedly free. But as recipients of the hemisphere's lowest wages, Cubans are paying higher than anyone for their medical care. Scarcity of medicines and medical supplies are blamed on the embargo despite the fact that Cuba could purchase its medical needs from any other country in the world where the cost would probably be lower than in the United States. The question arises why hospitals available to the population are so different from those available to tourists with dollars? If there is such scarcity [of medical supplies], why doesn't Cuba allow international organizations to distribute humanitarian aid with proper supervision and without government interference? How can Cuba advertise a medical tourism that can cure ailments of a privileged few when their own are not well taken care of? Because Cuba is true to the Marxist maxim:

"the end justifies the means," and it is dollars that Fidel Castro desperately needs to keep his repressive apparatus alive and his grip on power strong.

The beginning of the Cuban Revolution was marked by an unprecedented wave of killings before the firing squad. It was "revolutionary justice" they explained. What should we call it when a tugboat is sunk in the bay of Havana with children on board (July 13, 1994) simply for trying to escape Castro's inferno. It was rammed into, and forceful power hoses swept babies from their mother's protective embrace. Finally the tugboat was sunk by government vessels, which watched as forty-two men, women, and children drowned. Those who lived told their story back in 1994, but it did not make front-page news. They told it before the United Nation's Human Rights Commission in Geneva and they told it before the U.S. Congress, but few were willing to listen. Not until the pope's visit in January 1998 did ABC's *Nightline* describe that event for the general public. Ted Koppel's introduction could not have been more eloquent: "It was an incident that went all but unnoticed by the U.S. media. The Cuban-American community protested, but they protest a lot and as I said, we in the mainstream media all but ignored it."

Yet those who insist on defending Fidel Castro do so in spite of the fact that not one of his so-called achievements could justify forty years of crimes, human-rights abuses, and lack of freedom. It would be like saying Hitler's killings were justified because Germany's economy was thriving.

We as exiles have also had to pay a terrible price. We have not only lost our country and been separated from our families. In addition Cuba has tried to discredit us and label us as intolerants and extremists. Our crime is passionately wanting for Cuba, democracy, freedom, and justice.

Those who serve as apologists for a dictatorship of forty years should stop blaming everyone else and have Castro hold free and democratic elections that will give the Cuban people the possibility to choose their own destiny. They should demand that Castro abolish political crimes and demand that he allow the free flow of expression that is the pillar of every democracy.

I watched in astonishment as a CNN report on the Cuban revolution's fortieth birthday discussed succession after Castro as if it were a dynastic matter. What about the will of the people? Why blame the Cuban American community for taking a tough stand against a dictatorship? Why blame Washington for not having diplomatic relations with a country that violates human rights? That they have relations with China is not the answer. Economic endeavors will never justify the deaths of freedom-loving students in Tiananmen Square. Let American tourists remember that when they are tempted to travel to paradisiac beaches enticed by photos of Cuban teen-age girls prostituting themselves for a few dollars.

The CNN report closed with Fidel Castro's famous words in 1953, before assuming power, as he was tried for attacking a military garrison in Santiago. "Go ahead, condemn me, history will absolve me!" I wish in all fairness that CNN would have told its millions of viewers that those words were not Castro's, but Hitler's, whom he deeply admired then. The book they are contained in, *Mein Kamf*, was Castro's source of inspiration during his university days. Despots have a lot in common; their minds and their deeds follow the same twisted path imposing their will by force. It is up to us to decide whether we become their willing executors.

~~~ ~~~ ~~~ ~~~ ~~~ ~~~ ~~~ ~~~ ~~~ ~~~ ~~~ ~~~ ~~~ ~~~ ~~~
~~~ ~~~ ~~~ ~~~ ~~~ ~~~ ~~~ ~~~ ~~~ ~~~ ~~~ ~~~ ~~~ ~~~ ~~~

Exile Dialogue with Cuba

Over the years, many exiles, especially in the younger generation, became more open to conversation with Cubans and the Cuban government on behalf of closer relations, although many were afraid to speak out for fear of terrorist retaliation. In November 1978 Castro proposed a dialogue between Cuba and Cubans outside the island. In response the exiles formed a "Committee of 75" to represent the Cuban community abroad (an estimated 1.2 million). Two sessions of the dialogue between the committee and Cuban officials took place in Havana in November and December 1978. Out of these meetings came a three-point agreement: Cuba promised to release three thousand political prisoners (more than 80 percent of the total) plus six hundred other prisoners at the rate of four hundred a month, do its part toward reuniting members of separated families, and allow Cubans abroad to visit relatives in Cuba. But the next year, two participants in the Dialogue—Carlos Múñiz Varela, owner of a travel agency in Puerto Rico that organized trips to Cuba, and Eulalio José Negrin, director of a Cuban immigrant center in Union City, were assassinated. Omega 7 claimed responsibility (Franklin, *Cuba and the United States*, pp. 151, 155; Baker, *Cuba Handbook*, pp. 44–45).

The next chapter in this official dialogue did not take place until 1994, when two hundred Cubans living abroad, mostly in the United States, accepted Cuba's invitation to a conference in Havana. Four points came out of this meeting:

1. Cuba will encourage visits and investments by the 1.5 million emigrants in the United States.
2. Legal emigrants will no longer have to wait five years before being allowed to return to visit or have to spend money in government-owned hotels.

3. The Cuban Foreign Ministry will establish a special office for dealing with the needs of emigrant Cubans and will publish a new magazine for them.
4. A limited number of children of emigrants will be allowed to study in Cuba.

In November 1995, at a second conference in Havana, Cuba announced that émigrés could apply for travel documents, renewable every two years, that would allow them to enter and leave Cuba whenever they chose.

Meanwhile, several groups in the United States have sought to further dialogue and reconciliation: Cambio Cubano, Cuban Committee for Democracy, Cuban American Committee for Peace, Antonio Maceo Brigade, Venceremos Brigade, Radio Progreso (in Miami), Casa de las Americas, and Center for Cuban Studies (in New York).

EXODUS OF ATHLETES

During this past decade a new kind of exodus has been taking place—a mini-emigration of Cuban athletes, primarily baseball players—to the United States, where they have joined major league teams and signed multi-million dollar contracts. This exodus has been the project of Joe Cubas, a Miami-born sports agent whose parents were émigrés. His goal has been to help Cuban athletes escape to the Dominican Republic or Costa Rica, where they can sign contracts with U.S. teams as free agents.

In one of the most recent cases, Orlando Hernández and seven others in January 1998 took a small sailboat to the Bahamas, where they requested political asylum in the United States. Eventually, Hernández and two others were cleared for humanitarian and "gifted talents" reasons to enter the United States. U.S authorities believed that Hernández, who had already been banned from Cuban baseball for helping others to defect, faced almost certain reprisal if he were sent home. Joe Cubas than sent a chartered plane to Nassau to pick up Hernández and his party and fly them to Costa Rica. Before the end of the year, Hernández had helped the New York Yankees win the World Series. Some of the baseball players Cubas has helped emigrate are Osvaldo Fernandez, Livan Hernández, Orlando (El Duque) Hernández, Rey Ordoñez, Vladamir Nuñez, and Larry Rodriguez.

Their defections have been a great sorrow to Cubans. All the athletes were the beneficiaries of a strong national sports program available to the Cuban people free of charge as one of the benefits of the revolution. Cubans had consistently had winning baseball teams at the Olympics. To have these athletes turn their backs on the system that has nurtured them in order to embrace a capitalist system of sports for huge individual wealth that does not benefit all was a profound disappointment.

"YOU CAN'T GO HOME AGAIN"

Most of the early émigrés had hoped to return to Cuba after a short interval and to resume life as before. As time went on, they still had the dream of returning, but the reality of the good life in the United States became the more powerful vision and influence. Many quickly adjusted. To most, the bit of paper decreeing ownership of Cuban land and resources was no longer a sure thing, although the U.S. government's continuing demand for compensation payment with interest for all the past years conjured up dreams of additional wealth. Moreover, the second and third generation of these émigrés, growing up in the United States and often knowing no Spanish, think of the United States as home.

Later émigrés were glad to escape the pain and suffering of Cuba under the blockade, but they soon discovered in the United States that health care and a good education were no longer rights to be enjoyed by all but privileges for those with wealth. Many found it hard to earn a living and learned that there was great pain and suffering in the United States, too (see box).

Two Émigrés of the Fourth Wave

Fulgencio Ferrer, born the son of a rural school teacher in Oriente Province in 1954, and Dalia Abrer, born in 1953 in Las Villas, were children when the revolution broke out. They met at the University of Havana, where he was studying physics and she was studying to be a dental technician. They were married in 1978. Fulgencio worked as a radiation control specialist for various medical-diagnostic centers in Havana and other provinces, and Dalia worked as a dental technician and became active in Ebenezer Baptist Church.

The latter part of the 1980s were rough years for the couple. The blockade was causing all kinds of shortages, their car was vandalized, and Dalia was having a series of miscarriages. Fulgencio felt that Cuba in its rectification process was not going far enough—that there needed to be more popular participation in the political decision making, more independence from the Soviet Union, and more openness in the government around Fidel Castro. In 1991, while attending a church convention in the United States, the couple decided to remain in Miami. Neither Fulgencio nor Dalia was able to find a job utilizing his or her professional skills. Fulgencio finally went to work on the production line in a Motorola factory, a job he found stressful and unsatisfying. The happiest event for them in 1992 was the birth of a daughter, Priscilla.

Fulgencio and Dalia now live in Atlanta, where he works for the Georgia Department for Human Services and she teaches in a church daycare center, still not work for which they had been trained. They have been granted permanent residency and have applied for citizenship. The couple returned to Cuba for a visit in 1998. They still feel guilty about leaving their families and church in Cuba and feel strongly that the United States should be more open to Cuba. They believe Cubans now have more freedom but also less money. At the same time they are sad that Cuban society seems to have become more individualistic, and they hope that the social gains of the revolution, and its concern for others, are not lost.

Both of these groups look at Cuba today from different historical perspectives, but they sense there can be no return to what they knew before. One can try to step back into the same river, but in many ways it has now become a different river—different water, a different hospitality to its lifeforms, a different current. For one thing, the collapse of the Soviet bloc has ended the fear of communism and Soviet attack. For another, there is a massive part of the population in Cuba that does not want to give up the values and benefits that the revolution has brought them. They see those values and benefits lacking in the United States and fear that the United States wants Cuba to give them up. They see themselves located somewhere between heaven and hell and believe that sovereignty means walking a risky, tenuous, self-determining path between the two.

And so the challenge before the divided Cuban community— those on the island and those scattered abroad—comes down to how to listen and talk to each other in creative dialogue, how to find reconciliation and be family together, and how to celebrate life and fiesta together.

Questions for Reflection

1. Imagine that you are a second-generation émigré living in New York. Your parents keep telling you how wonderful life was in Cuba before the revolution. But they don't plan to move back because they have negative feelings about Cuba and they have grown used to the freedom and comfort of life in the United States. You have joined a college group that advocates reconciliation and has invited you to join a work brigade for a month in Cuba. You want to go, but your parents would be very angry. What do you do?

2. Imagine that you were a rich sugar magnate in Cuba before the revolution. You are now an even richer businessman in Florida. Why are you

pressing the U.S. government to keep up the blockade? If the Cuban government changed, would you go back?

3. Put yourself in the place of an émigré who escaped Cuba on a raft to look for a better life in Miami. As a person of few skills, no English, and no health insurance, you are having a rough time in the United States. How does Cuba look to you now? Would you go back?

4. Make believe that your sister and her rich husband emigrated to Miami, while you stayed behind to look after your old mother. They visit you yearly, bringing you new clothes and money to buy new electronic equipment. But your apartment is crumbling, frequent electrical black-outs curtail the use of your television, and such necessities as a battery for your old car are hard to find. How do you feel about your sister and brother-in-law?

5. To many émigrés the unforgivable sin of the Cuban revolution is its more equitable redistribution of the island's wealth to include the poor blacks, and women. Is such redistribution basically un-Cuban, un-American, undemocratic?

CHAPTER 5

CUBANS AND NORTH AMERICANS: STEWARDS TOGETHER

T he last five hundred years of Cuban history have been a chronicle of struggle marked by frustration and accomplishment, sorrow and joy, suffering and hope. Could Cuba's sixth century possibly become a new era of Good Neighbor policies and peace?

The challenge of creating such a future is formidable. For the last four decades the United States has been conducting an undeclared war against Cuba and its people. The United States has also erected a great Sea Wall—a barrier between itself and Cuba that has hindered travel, understanding, and empathy. As a result, most U.S. residents know little about life in Cuba, and that little is often heavily colored by the media. For example, in the *New York Times* of November 8, 1998, Larry Rother compared the responses of three Caribbean nations to Hurricane Georges:

In Puerto Rico, an American possession, the government leaped into action as soon as the first hurricane watch was issued. Television stations reportedly broadcast warnings to stay indoors and put up hurricane shutters, provided advice on stockpiling food and water, and showed footage of past storms to remind the island's 3.5 million residents of what they might face. As soon as Georges passed, utility repair crews were out restoring service and Federal Emergency Management Agency teams were preparing reports and sending money.

Next door in the Dominican Republic, disorganization was the watchword. Newspapers there have complained that the civil defense chief, Elpidio Baez, failed to issue storm warnings because he did not want to alarm people. . . . Some people who went to hurricane shelters found them closed and were turned away by soldiers.

The hurricane then moved on to Cuba, which, true to form for a militarized totalitarian state, responded as if the storm were an enemy to be vanquished.

President Fidel Castro instructed residents of affected zones to evacuate, an order that was enforced by the military and local security watchdogs and may have saved many lives. Afterwards the Communist Party newspaper *Granma* praised Cubans for their "revolutionary discipline" and successful "combat" against Georges, whose "destructive force" amounted to a "kind of invasion."

Rother did not point out similarities between U.S. actions in Puerto Rico and Castro's actions in Cuba. Nor did he mention how residents on the southern coast of the United States were also given instructions to evacuate, and how they were helped to do so by military and law enforcement officials.

This alienation and enmity between the two countries raises important questions for Christians. How can the dividing wall of hostility be broken down? How can these troubled waters be bridged? One place to begin would be to think through (with Cubans, if possible) what it would mean for North Americans and Cubans to live together in a common household, as stewards of that household. The Greek word *oikos*, meaning "house" or "household," provides a helpful jumping off point for such a discussion, because three important words derive from that root word: *economic, ecological,* and *ecumenical.* They refer to three crucial areas in which we live out our calling as stewards. If peace and reconciliation are at all attainable in this new century, it will be through nations and individuals acting justly, loving gently, and walking humbly together in these three areas. The *oikos* concept and its implication for stewardship are spelled out further in two recent books: *God the Economist: The Doctrine of God and Political Economy* by M. Douglas Meeks (1989), and *Earth Community, Earth Ethics* by Larry L. Rasmussen (1996).

ECONOMIC SPHERE

Economy concerns the way we manage or organize the household we live in, especially in terms of the production, distribution, and consumption of goods and services. The key word in this sphere is *justice.* According to Meeks, *oikos* is the household in which God wants to give people access to life. God's work is to make the world into such a household, and the church is God's attempt to gain help in that work. The basic question of economy is, "Will everyone in the household receive what it takes to live?"

Meeks goes on to describe ways in which oppressive forms of *oikos* restrict this access. Racism and sexism are deeply embedded in most economic systems. And in an economy predominately defined by market arrangements, as in Western societies, the domination of nature through technology and the eclipsing of participatory politics by the values and mechanisms of the market are additional forms of oppression. It is in the economic area that the greatest difference between the United States and

Cuba occurs—a conflict between two organizing principles: in capitalism, the maximization of profit; in socialism, the meeting of human needs. Given the probability that these two competing systems will continue to exist for sometime, there are nevertheless a number of issues of justice confronting us that will need to be solved if we are to break down the dividing wall of hostility and find reconciliation. The following suggestions are possible solutions.

Return Guantánamo

Because Cuba was forced to cede Guantánamo to the United States as a condition for ending the U.S. occupation, U.S. control of Guantánamo, according to international law, is an illegal occupation of Cuba's sovereign territory. Today the base no longer has the same military or geographical importance for the United States that it had at the beginning of the century. Its greater importance today is ideological: this foreign control of Cuban territory against the wishes of Cuba is a grating symbol of Cuba's powerlessness. In a time when the Panama Canal Zone has been returned to Panama and Hong Kong returned to China it would seem that Guantánamo's return to Cuba is long overdue.

End the Blockade and Other Acts of War

The forty-year-old U.S. economic blockade has cost Cuba an estimated $50 billion, forcing it to obtain food, medical supplies, and other necessities from long distances and at higher prices. The years of terrorist attacks by paramilitary groups and individuals and U.S. efforts to destabilize, infiltrate, and invade Cuba have kept Cuba from relaxing its tight wartime control over civil liberties and dissent, much of the latter supported and funded by the United States.

The UN General Assembly has for a number of years declared the blockade against Cuba a violation of the UN charter and international law, freedom of trade, and the sovereignty of other states. The assembly, taking special note of the blockade's adverse effects on the Cuban people and on Cuban nationals, has called for the lifting of this blockade.

Because Congress, under pressure from constituents to maintain the blockade, has taken the responsibility of foreign policy relating to Cuba out of the President's hands, it will now be much harder to change this policy. But there are signs of new initiatives. At the end of 1998 Senator John Warner from Virginia, joined by Henry Kissinger, Lawrence Eagleburger, and other Republicans formerly associated with the State Department, called for a bipartisan commission to reexamine U.S. policy toward Cuba, including trade barriers and the domestic and international impact of the blockade.

It remains to be seen whether this proposal is an attempt to change U.S. policy in order to ameliorate conditions within Cuba or is part of the "Track Two" strategy of the Torricelli Law: seeking greater entry into Cuba in order to sow discord among the Cuban people so that they will ultimately replace their government. Kissinger's track record of destabilizing the Allende government of Chile in 1970–73, the Manley government of Jamaica in 1972–80, and other operations would seem to indicate the latter.

Agree on Compensation

When Cuba offered compensation over a twenty-year period for U.S.-owned properties that had been nationalized, the United States refused. Since then, it has criticized Cuba for not paying compensation. In December 1996 the National Assembly once again ratified Cuba's willingness to negotiate compensation, asking only that it be done on a basis of equality and mutual respect and take into account Cuban claims related to the effects of the blockade and U.S. aggression since 1960, an estimated $50 billion.

Protect the Gains of the Revolution

Cubans take pride in the gains of the revolution: free health care and education; the virtual elimination of malnutrition, poverty, gambling, corruption, racial and gender discrimination, and a high infant mortality rate; one of the most highly educated populations in Latin America; and the opportunity for citizens of modest means to be elected to public office. Even more important in their eyes are the values instilled by the revolution: the importance of caring for one another, of meeting human need both at home and abroad, of not letting anyone fall through the cracks, of striving for social and economic justice. Cubans do not want to lose these gains as they make new economic arrangements to survive the pressures of "free market" economics in the midst of the twin blows of the blockade and the demise of the socialist bloc.

These accomplishments and values have come under continuing attack from the United States. As mentioned in chapter 4, the Clinton administration in 1997 published a report that calls for the privatization of the Cuban health and education systems, public services and utilities, and banks and industries, and a transition to a political economy similar to the one in the United States.

As U.S. citizens enter into dialogue with our Cuban sisters and brothers, we need to ask ourselves a number of important questions: Do we really want the Cubans to have an economic system like ours where 30 million citizens are hungry, between 5 and 7 million are homeless, and more than 40 million have no health insurance? Do we really want Cuba, which maintains that "Nothing is more important than a child," to become more like the United States, which has the highest rate of child poverty of any industrialized nation—one in every five children?

Do we really want the Cuban educational system to be funded by local property taxes, which in United States vary

Day care, medical attention, and school for all children are among the gains of the revolution that Cubans want to preserve.

widely (for instance, in Texas during 1991–92, spending ranged from $2,337 per pupil in the poorest district to $56,791 in the wealthiest)? Do we really want Cuba to reinstate gambling and lotteries, which target the poor, as a way to help pay for its schools?

Do we really want Cuba to adopt the U.S. electoral system, in which during the 1998 midterm elections more than $1 billion was spent to elect a House and Senate that changed only slightly, and in which the candidates with the most money won 92 percent of House races and 88 percent of Senate races? In the 1996 electoral campaign, the average victor spent about $4.5 million for a Senate seat and more than $500,000 for a House seat. Do we really want Cuba to have a lobbying industry similar to the one in the United States, which spends $100 million a month lobbying members in Congress, or $187,000 per month per member?

Do we really want the profit from privatized companies in Cuba to go into astronomical CEO salaries and the pockets of stockholders in the United States? In short will the changes our government proposes help our brothers and sisters in Cuba obtain what it takes to live?

ECOLOGICAL SPHERE

Ecology is the study of the way organisms interrelate with one another and with their environment for the mutual upbuilding of harmonious life systems. The key word in this sphere is *shalom* (health, wholeness, peace). Meeks describes *oikos* as the household of creation in which God wants all creatures to live together in a mutually beneficial relationship. Such a symbiosis is built into the human ecology of Cuba in several important ways.

Mutually beneficial relationships are nurtured at the most basic level of society, as described in chapter 4, through the neighborhood block organizations, the CDRs. Originally designed for defending the neighborhood against sabotage, they soon evolved into organizations to undergird the health, welfare, and caring relationships of the residents, and provide a channel for feedback and action on behalf of the larger society.

Working closely with each CDR are the neighborhood family doctor, social worker, and nurse. This holistic neighborhood unit is backed up by the free national health-care system, another symbol to the Cuban people of a society that has been organized for their benefit. Neighborhood block organizations and health-care units are stewardship ideas that the United States and Canada could pick up from Cuba, to help increase social cohesiveness and well-being in each community. U.S. medical practitioners have already discovered that an active neighborhood support group can have a profound effect on the physical and psychological health of a community.

Another notable feature of Cuba's human ecology is the high degree of racial diversity. Cuba's mixed population is perhaps the most integrated in Latin America. Columbus wrote in his diary about the tremendous beauty of the island. He could never have appreciated Cuba's new beauty, a people in a rainbow of hues. Their dignity, self-assurance, and self-confidence are one of the most important achievements of the revolution.

Symbiosis is present in Cuba in another special way—its highly developed environmental ecology. In order to cope with the blockade and a life of scarcity, Cuba has turned the whole country into an experiment with organic agriculture, herbal medicine, and natural energy sources, a process described by Peter Rosset and Medea Benjamin in their book and video titled *The Greening of the Revolution* (1994). They tell about Cuba's national effort to preserve the environment through the use of organic fertilizers and crop rotation; biological control of pests; biological cycles and seasonality of crops and animals; energy from water, wind, the sun, slopes, and biomass; animal traction, rational use of pastures for grazing and feedlots, and local sources of animal nutrition.

Cuba is also recovering herbal medicines that were used by the indigenous people centuries ago. Every family doctor cultivates an herbal garden in the clinic yard. Such medicines, however, still do not compensate for foreign medicine unobtainable because of the blockade. These "green agriculture" and "green medicine" developments are important for the whole human family and should be shared among the members of the global household. In a sense, the industrialized world is being challenged to reclaim the reverence for life and harmonious relationship with creation that characterized the Tainos in their earliest years of Cuba.

Human and environmental ecology has now become a national priority of Cuba, according to a law passed by the National Assembly in 1997. The law addresses such issues in the scientific-technical sphere as a means of attaining sustainable development, the role of environmental education, the link between the environment and cultural heritage, the relation of issues to the workplace, administrative and penal responsibility for environment damage, and the fulfillment of international agreements.

ECUMENICAL SPHERE

Ecumenical refers to the whole inhabited world, the household of faith. It has also come to refer to worldwide Christian unity—the faith that embraces the whole world and all its inhabitants in its concern. The key word in this ecumenical sphere is *unity*.

Meeks notes that *oikos* refers to the world that God wants to make into a home by establishing justice and peace among the people. The question of ecumenism is, "Will all people be able to live in the world as a home?"

Ecumenical Relations

Churches and individual Christians in the United States and Canada have maintained close ecumenical ties with the churches in Cuba through visits, study seminars, work camps, partner-church relationships, and shipments of humanitarian aid. The aid has been sent through two main channels: Church World Service, an arm of the National Council of Churches, and Pastors for Peace, founded in 1988 by the Baptist pastor Lucius Walker. Church World Service obtains a license from the U.S. Treasury for its shipments. Pastors for Peace refuses to apply for a license, believing that the U.S. government has no right to control church aid and that it would mean complicity with the blockade. Both channels are important avenues for Christian witness.

Since 1992 Church World Service has sent more than forty-four plane loads of food; medicine and medical equipment; school, health, and sewing kits; blankets; soap; and other goods, with a value of some $8 million. This aid has been distributed through the Cuban Council of Churches.

Yellow school bus given by Minneapolis to Pastors for Peace was impounded at the border by U.S. customs officials before it was finally released.

Since 1992 eight Pastors for Peace caravans have collected aid from various parts of the United States and Canada, sending eight "Friendshipments" to Cuba to be distibuted through the Martin Luther King, Jr., Center of the Ebenezer Church. This aid has included medical and dental equipment, medicines, powered milk, school supplies, Bibles, equipment for children with physical disabilities, computers, bicycles, school buses, and an ambulance. Because of the lack of a license there have been a number of confrontations with the U.S. government at the border. In July 1993 a little yellow school bus was seized by U.S. authorities, but after a twenty-three-day hunger strike by caravaners, it was released and delivered to Cuba. In March 1994 U.S. officials seized communication equipment but finally released it. In January 1996, hospitals, churches, and individuals from nineteen U.S. West Coast cities and Canada donated more than 350 computers for INFOMED, the Cuban electronic medical sciences information network linking Cuban hospitals, research centers, medical schools, and rural clinics. This project was sponsored by the Cuban Council of Churches, King Center, Brotherhood of Cuban Baptist Churches, Christian Student Movement, Christian Medical Commission, and many other Christian organizations in Cuba. After the computers were seized by U.S. customs, four members of Pastors for Peace began a "Fast for Life" that lasted for ninety-four days. The U.S. government finally capitulated and released the computers to the United Methodist Church, which transferred them to Cuba.

U.S. Methodists in the Florida Conference have renewed their relationship with the Cuban Methodist church. U.S. Methodists in Florida, Georgia, and Cleveland gave $49,000 to buy nine thousand Spanish-language hymnals from the United Methodist Publishing House at a special price to send to Cuban Methodists. Since the books could not go directly through the blockade, a Canadian firm agreed to ship them.

Not all members of the household of faith in the United States support such humanitarian aid to Cuba. Representative Robert Torricelli from New Jersey, a United Methodist, told a Cuba study group at Georgetown University. "I want to wreak havoc on that island. . . . I want to bring down Fidel Castro." The authors of the Helms-Burton Act, Jesse Helms and Dan Burton, are also church members.

The Jubilee Year and Cancellation of Debt

One of the most powerful images in the Bible is that of Jubilee. Every fifty years there is to be a granting of freedom—to people being held in bondage to slavery or debt, and also to land being exploited (Lev. 25:8–25, Deut. 15:1–18). Jesus picked up this Jubilee theme from Isaiah 61:1–2 when he began his ministry in Nazareth (Luke 4:18–19), and when he included the cancellation of debt in the prayer he taught his disciples (Luke 11:1–4). Fidel Castro has been concerned with the cancellation of Third World debt. In March 1985, he declared in an interview, "There's no other choice: the cancellation of the debt or the political death of the democratic process in Latin America," and in an address to Latin American journalists in July 1985, he claimed, "This debt is not only unpayable but also uncollectible." The fact that Third World countries owe huge amounts in interest, even though they have repaid the principal, is the perfect plan for keeping a nation in perpetual bondage. Many of the original loans were made back in the 1970s by Northern banks to undemocratic civilian and military governments. The money went primarily into the pockets of the elite; yet today the poor are being forced to bear the repayment costs because the International Monetary Fund will not grant a new loan to cover the interest on the old loans unless the debtor nation agrees to make major cuts in social programs and spending, privatize state-owned enterprises, and increase export crops and trade.

In October 1997 Sergio Arce, Cuban Presbyterian theologian and former rector of the Evangelical Seminary at Matanzas, in an address to The United Church of Canada, spelled out the harsh reality of the international debt:

> During the last ten years the poor countries of this world have nurtured the economy of the rich with more than five hundred billions of U.S. dollars. This is

equivalent to twice the Marshall Plan. During the last thirty years the developed rich countries have increased their wealth threefold; in ten years the Latin American countries have transferred to the rich countries of the world about two hundred fifty billion U.S. dollars solely in payment of the interest on their external debts that total five hundred billion.

An external debt that is impossible to pay back means that the Latin American countries have fallen into the most complete dependence in relation to international banks and the rich industrialized and developed countries. The debt that cannot be paid corrodes society, works against social stability, political auto-determination, and sustainable development. It implies the sacrifice of human beings on the altar of a contemporary Moloch, a new God, like the old Mammon.

The most striking example of what I am saying is found in the changes in the translation of the Lord's Prayer to our modern languages. Now we do not pray as Jesus taught us: "And forgive our debts as we also have forgiven our debtors," according to St. Matthew's Gospel. . . .To talk of "forgiving debts" as a condition for God's forgiveness is too much for those who want to collect them anyway. It is much easier to change a sacred text. [*Ed. note: Many churches retain "debts" and "debtors" in the Lord's Prayer.*]

Today many U.S. Christians are planning to join Christians in other parts of the world to celebrate Jubilee-2000—an ecumenical program that calls for applying the biblical principle of Jubilee to economic issues and especially to the international debt. This idea is beginning to catch on in secular circles, as well. In June 1998 the thousand-member U.S. Conference of Mayors at its annual meeting adopted a resolution that "calls upon the President and Congress to provide leadership in working toward significant debt reduction and cancellation of debt owed by the poorest African countries to the world's richest industrial nations."

Cuba has had a hard time trying to make any headway on its debt to thirteen creditors (Austria, Belgium, Britain, Canada, Denmark, France, Germany, Italy, Japan, the Netherlands, Spain, Sweden, and Switzerland) because of the blockade and being closed out of world markets. Several times it has rescheduled some $1.2 billion of its debt. In 1994 Cuba and Mexico signed an oil and telephone agreement that canceled Cuba's $340 million debt to Mexico. In 1995 Cuba sought to restructure an estimated $64.4 billion in hard-currency debt, owed to Western countries and Japan. Even in the midst of this hardship, Cuba sought to carry out its own principle of debt cancellation. In November 1998, in response to the devastation caused by Hurricane Mitch, Cuba forgave the $50 million debt Nicaragua owed Cuba.

There are a few examples of debt forgiveness by the United States. Noam Chomsky lists several. When the United States took over Cuba a hundred years ago, it canceled Cuba's debt to Spain on the grounds that the burden was "imposed upon the people of Cuba without their consent and by force of arms." Later when Britain, France, and Italy defaulted on U.S. debts in the 1930s, Washington forgave them.

The Earth Charter

An important document for Cubans and North Americans to discuss together in terms of their common task of stewardship is the Earth Charter. Part of an international movement to develop a new global ethics, it reflects the conviction that a radical change in humanity's values is essential to achieve social, economic, and ecological well-being in the twenty-first century. A final draft is to be adopted in the year 2000.

The charter begins by listing three general principles: 1. Respect Earth and all life. 2. Care for Earth's community of life in all its diversity. 3. Create global partnership and secure justice, peace, and Earth's abundance and beauty for present and future generations. It then goes on to list nine ecological, economic, and social principles, and then nine guidelines for implementing sustainability.

The document can be obtained from the Earth Charter Drafting Committee, c/o Steven Rockefeller, P.O. Box 648, Middlebury, VT 05753.

The charter provides a stimulating basis for conversation between North Americans and Cubans and suggests areas of cooperation and solidarity. Such conversation between Columbus and the Tainos might have made a big difference in the history of the last five hundred years. At least the present-day decendants of European, Taino, and African immigrants can begin the conversation now.

AN INVITATION TO FURTHER STUDY AND ACTION

It is hoped that readers of this book will have gained some new kinds of information, perspectives, and lenses that will be helpful in our common task as stewards on behalf of justice, shalom, and unity. Following are a number of ideas for next steps. Full information on the suggested books and organizations is given in the section "Resources."

Learn More About Cuba

Two conversations make for fascinating reading—the one between Juan Antonio Blanco and Medea Benjamin in *Talking About Revolution,* and the one between Fidel Castro and Frei Betto in *Fidel and Religion.* Three periodicals—*CubaInfo, Cuba Update,* and *Granma International*—provide current news about Cuba. In addition, a person with a shortwave radio can tune in to Radio Havana broadcasts in English every evening.

Three resources challenge the viewer or reader to move to deeper level of empathy and compassion: the videos *Soy Cubano!* and *Cuba Calls*

. . . *We Must Answer* and the American Association for World Health report, *Denial of Food and Medicine*.

Send Humanitarian Aid

Individuals or groups can help send food, medicine, medical supplies, school supplies, and other aid to Cuba. Send money to Church World Service, to be converted into relief. Call Pastors for Peace to find out the dates and itineraries for their next caravans—they can send down computers for Cuba's health system. Ben Treuhaft, founder of the Send a Piana to Havana project, welcomes contributions of pianos and cash for replacement strings, felts, and action parts, and also to send down piano technicians and tuners (contributions are tax-deductible).

Change U.S. Policy

As various bills to revise or abolish the blockade are presented in Congress, it will be important for U.S. citizens to be in contact with representatives and senators. Watch newspapers, magazines, *CubaInfo*, and other resources. Two U.S. representatives from New York, Charles B. Rangel, 2354 Rayburn House Office Building, Washington, DC 20515. Tel. (202) 225-4365, fax (202) 225-0861, and Jose E. Serrano, 2342

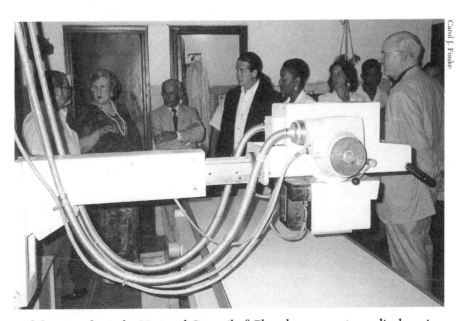

Carol J. Fouke

A delegation from the National Council of Churches presents medical equipment donated by two California Rotary Clubs in collaboration with Direct Relief International to the Antonio Guiteras Holms Polyclinic in Havana. The NCC plans to send a new X-ray machine to replace the old one.

Rayburn House Office Building, Washington, DC 20515. Tel. (202) 225-4361, fax (202) 225-6001, have been strong supporters of lifting the embargo. It would be good to get on their mailing list for legislative alerts.

Visit Cuba

There is no better way to become acquainted with Cuba and its people than by visiting there in person—talking with Cubans on the street, in their homes, at work, at church. Call or write the Latin America office of your mission board to find out what kinds of opportunities it offers for visiting Cuba. Other possibilities are listed in "Resources."

There are several important topics for discussion between North Americans and Cubans: What it means to be members or stewards of a common household; what the challenge of Jubilee is for both peoples; what ratifying the Earth Charter would mean; what the implications of turning arms into tools of food production are for each country.

Rev. Joan Brown Campbell, head of the NCC, meets the director of the Guiteras Polyclinic in June 1998.

Establish a Partner-Church Relationship

An exciting relationship of sharing and fellowship can develop between a North American and a Cuban congregation in the form of an exchange of personal letters, church newsletters, study resources, banners and art work, visits. It is important, however that this relationship be kept nonfinancial (except for helping to pay for the visits of Cubans). Call or write your denomination's Latin American office or the Cuban Council of Churches for suggestions: Address: Calle 14 #304 e/3 y 5, Miramar 11200, Havana, Cuba. Tel. (011-53-7) 23-7791, fax (011-53-7) 24-1788, E-mail: iglesias@mail.infocom.etecsa.cu

Establish a Sister Cities Relationship

A partnership between cities, inaugurated by city council resolutions, can lead to many creative interrelationships between universities, schools, hospitals, corporations, and other organizations. There are official sister city ties between Pittsburgh and Matanzas and between Mobile and Havana. Ties are developing between Madison, Wisconsin, and Camagüey; San Francisco and Santiago de Cuba; Bloomington, Indiana, and Santa Clara; and Philadelphia and Santiago de Cuba. For further information, write or call Lisa Valanti, president of the U.S.-Cuba Sister Cities Association, 320 Lowenhill St., Pittsburgh, PA 15216. Tel. (412) 563-1519, fax (412) 563-1945, E-mail: lisacubasi@aol.com

Questions for Reflection

1. The United States refuses to lift the blockade on Cuba, although it is against international law and the UN has voted to end it for the last five years. How do you justify the U.S. position?
2. Tourism brings Cuba much-needed dollars, but it also brings a two-tier economy and encourages prostitution. Do you think the benefits outweigh the evils? What other solutions might there be?
3. "Nothing is more important than a child" is an important saying in Cuba, which spends a large part of its budget on children's health and education. Why do the United States and Canada not put children first? What would it mean if we did?
4. In order to cope with the scarcities caused by the blockade, Cuba has experimented with organic agriculture, herbal medicine, natural energy, and animal power. How could such measures benefit the United States and Canada? Since a prosperous economy and plentiful resources benefit everyone, why are business people and ecologists usually at war?

THE PROBLEM AND RECONCILIATION

Walter Brueggemann states in his book *A Social Reading of the Old Testament: Prophetic Approaches to Israel's Communal Life* (1994), "Justice is a social question about social power and social access, about agreed-upon systems and practices of social production, distribution, possession, and consumption." In this book on Cuba we have been looking at different ways in which people and nations related to Cuba over the past five centuries have chosen social values and organized societies. They have found different answers to basic questions: Who should have access to power and to the social benefits of a system and who should not? Who should be able to own and control land, natural resources, and the wealth these produce? Who gets to decide? At the deepest level, such questions are theological because each of these systems of social values and organization is supported and legitimated by a certain concept of "God." To some, God is an ultimate authority that blesses the unequal benefits of a society. To others, God hears the cries of the poor and oppressed and blesses their efforts to obtain justice.

U.S. currency carries an official credo: "In God We Trust." The theological content of this affirmation is not spelled out, but its placement on our principal medium of exchange is clear: our trust is in God who blesses our nation, legitimizes its individualistic economic and political system, and provides great wealth for some of its members. It is the same God that legitimized the Cuban system before 1959, and when a different system was inaugurated in Cuba that year, many people left for the North where the same familiar God was still authorizing a familiar kind of society. It should be noted, however, that some Cubans who moved to the United States joined the struggle there for greater justice.

It was common in Cuba before 1959, as it is still common in the United States today, for people of good will to deliver holiday baskets of food to the needy. On a recent Thanksgiving a Protestant pastor received the following note from a Jewish friend:

On this day, fight the impulses you have to give food at a homeless shelter . . .
on this day, DON'T buy a toy for tots for xmas . . .
on this day, don't send a check to a needy person . . .
on this day, don't visit a hospital's sick . . .
on this day, don't adopt a grandparent . . .

DON'T DO IT NOW, NOR DURING THE NEXT SIX WEEKS . . .
wait until the guilt has subsided
and then in a true act of justice
in the quiet of January
when the homeless have shifted from view
when the old people are once again forgotten
when shoes and jackets and gloves are needed, not a Barbie doll,
then get off your duff and DO something about the problem.

What *is* the problem that needs to be solved? Is it a problem of distribution? How is access to life to be determined in God's household? The organizing principle that determines the answer separates people to the north of the Straits of Florida from those to the south. One organizing principle is that distribution should be based on concern for the needs of all. Another is that distribution should be based on the merit of the successful few.

Brueggemann upholds the first principle, reminding us that for the prophets, "the advocacy of justice concerns both the social system and the God confessed through the practice of the social system." He also reminds us that the Bible urges an alternative reading of human community that can only be described as covenantal: "Property must be managed, valued, and distributed so that every person of the community is honored and so that the well-being of each is intimately tied to that of the others."

Another important insight into this prophetic perspective is given us in Robert Gnuse's book *You Shall Not Steal: Community and Property in the Biblical Tradition* (1985), "Property and land were given to be used for the glory of Yahweh and the good of all. The command not to steal spoke against those who sought to appropriate communal possessions for their own private use." He offers a re-reading of the eighth commandment: "Do not take communal property for your own individual ownership," and comments, "How ironic that modern society uses the commandment to defend the opposite course of action!"

129

Thus the Tainos and the ancient Hebrew prophets had a common perspective on property and on the communal values of love and sharing—one that the Cuban revolution has sought to incorporate into its modus operandi. It is especially interesting that Che Guevara's saying, "Truly, the life of a single human being is a million times more valuable than all the property of the richest man on earth," should be placed in a "shalom" setting—on a billboard at the entrance to the Calixto Garcia Hospital in Havana. It is a great irony that the two chief national "offspring" of the Hebrew Torah and the Christian Bible—Israel and the United States—are the only remaining defendants of the U.S. blockade of Cuba in the United Nations Assembly.

The other organizing principle, prevalent in the North, can also be called the "divine right of wealth." In 1976 the U.S. Supreme Court ruled in *Buckley vs. Valeo* that any infringement on campaign spending was an infringement of free speech, thus removing any limits on the power of the rich to use money to advance their electoral interests. (The majority of the nine Supreme Court justices are millionaires.) Such a principle would prevent people like Raúl Suárez from serving in the National Assembly.

Or is the problem to be solved that of how far a nation should go in the socializing process? The answer is another organizing principle that divides peoples. Cuba believes in socializing both the profits of business and the costs. In the United States corporate profits are considered private property, but costs are socialized among the whole population. Thus ailing corporations such as Lockheed, Chrysler, savings and loan institutions, and other nations are bailed out at public expense. Professional sports teams are given tax write-offs, and stadiums are built at public expense. There is a campaign to transfer public welfare institutions such as health care, education, prisons, and Social Security to the private sector, where they will benefit corporate profit.

These are all basic questions of social organization and stewardship that need to be solved. To do so, we desperately need as wide a sharing of experience, perspective, and wisdom as possible. Somehow, in this time of great estrangement and enmity between two nations, people of good will in the United States, Canada, and Cuba will need to carry out imaginative and effective strategies for breaking down the dividing wall of hostility in order to bring about a reconciled and united humanity.

The New England poet Robert Frost has spoken in "Mending Wall" about how in both nature and people there is a deep aversion to walls and how we need to know clearly what we are trying to wall in and wall out. Such knowledge is a crucial first step, but then comes the crucial second step, demolishing and removing the wall.

For people in the United States, I believe, reconciliation will mean, at some solemn and repentant point, making apology and amends to the Cuban people for the great pain and suffering caused by U.S. policy, and showing a willingness to let Cuba develop its own future. For Christians, reconciliation will mean plumbing the biblical claim that this breaking down of walls of hostility and reconciling has already taken place through the Prophet of Nazareth, the Announcer of Jubilee, the Healer of Brokenness, the Breaker of Purity Codes, the Overturner of Commodity Tables, the Criminal of Golgotha, and the One who walks with us along our Emmaus roads.

RESOURCES

BOOKS

Cuban History and Development

Arboleya, Jesus. *Havana-Miami: The U.S.-Cuba Migration Conflict*. Melbourne: Ocean Press, 1996.

Azicri, Max. *Cuba: Politics, Economics and Society*. London: Pinter, 1988.

Bigelow, Bill, et al., eds. *Rethinking Columbus*. Milwaukee: Rethinking Schools, 1991. (Rethinking Schools, 1001 E. Keefe Ave., Milwaukee, WI 53212.)

Blanco, Juan Antonio, and Medea Benjamin. *Cuba: Talking About Revolution*. Melbourne: Ocean Press, 1997.

Boorstein, Edward. *The Economic Transformation of Cuba*. New York: Modern Reader, 1968.

Brenner, Philip, et al., eds. *The Cuba Reader: The Making of Revolutionary Society*. New York: Grove Press, 1989.

Chomsky, Noam. *Year 501: The Conquest Continues*. Boston: South End Press, 1993.

Deutschmann, David. *Che Guevara Reader*. Melbourne: Ocean Press, 1997.

Frank, Marc. *Cuba Looks to the Year 2000*. New York: International Publishers Co., 1993.

Franklin, Jane. *Cuba and the United States: A Chronological History*. Melbourne: Ocean Press, 1997.

Garcia, Cristina. *Dreaming in Cuban*. New York: Ballantine Books, 1992. Fictional account of a Cuban family in Cuba and in exile in New York.

Garcia Luis, Julio. *Cuban Revolutionary Reader: A Documentary History*. Melbourne: Ocean Press, 1999.

Halebsky, Sandor, and John M. Kirk, eds. *Transformation and Struggle: Cuba Faces the 1990s*. New York: Praeger Publishers, 1990.

Johnson, John J. *Latin America Caricature*. Austin: University of Texas Press, 1980.

Kirk, John M. *José Martí: Mentor of the Cuban Nation*. Tampa: University Presses of Florida, 1983.

Kirk, John M., and Peter McKenna. *Canada-Cuba Relations: The Other Good Neighbor Policy*. Gainesville: University Presses of Florida, 1997.

Koning, Hans. *Columbus: His Enterprise*. New York: Monthly Review Press, 1976.

Kromer, Helen. *Amistad: The Slave Uprising Aboard the Spanish Schooner*. Cleveland: Pilgrim Press, 1997.

Muñiz, Mirta, and Pedro Alvarez Fabio. *Fidel Castro Reader: Forty Years of the Cuban Revolution*. Melbourne: Ocean Press, 1999.

Pérez, Louis A., Jr. *Cuba: Between Reform and Revolution*. New York: Oxford University Press, 1988.

———. *The War of 1898: The United States and Cuba in History and Historiography*. Chapel Hill: University of North Carolina Press, 1998.

Rius, Eduardo del Rio. *Cuba for Beginners*. New York: Pathfinder Press, 1978. A political cartoon history of Cuba.

Rosset, Peter, and Medea Benjamin. *The Greening of the Revolution: Cuba's Experiment with Organic Agriculture*. Melbourne: Ocean Press, 1994.

Ruffin, Patricia. *Capitalism and Socialism in Cuba: A Study of Dependency, Development, and Underdevelopment*. London: Macmillan, 1990.

Shnookal, Deborah, and Mirta Muñiz. *José Martí Reader: Writings on the Americas*. Melbourne: Ocean Press, 1999.

Simons, Geoff. *Cuba: From Conquistador to Castro*. London: Macmillan, 1996.

Smith, Wayne S., and Michael Reagan. *Portrait of Cuba*. Atlanta: Turner Publishing, 1991.

Stone, Elizabeth, ed. *Women and the Cuban Revolution*. New York: Pathfinder Press, 1981.

Tablada, Carlos. *Che Guevara: Economics and Politics in the Transition to Socialism*. Sydney: Pathfinder Books, 1989.

Thomas, Hugh. *Cuba or the Pursuit of Freedom*. New York: Da Capo Press, 1998.

Zinn, Howard: *A People's History of the United States: 1492–Present*. New York: Harper Perennial, 1995.

U.S. War Against Cuba

The large number of books in this section shows the amount of recent research and opening of government files on this subject.

American Association for World Health. *Denial of Food and Medicine: The Impact of the U.S. Embargo on Health & Nutrition in Cuba* (Executive Summary, March 1997). (AAWH, 1825 K. St. NW, Suite 1208, Washington, DC 20006.)

Blum, William. *Killing Hope: U.S. Military and CIA Interventions Since World War II*. Monroe, Me., Common Courage Press, 1995.

CIA Targets Fidel: Secret 1967 CIA Inspector General's Report on Plots to Assassinate Fidel Castro. Melbourne: Ocean Press, 1996.

Elliston, Jon. *Psywar on Cuba: History of U.S. Anti-Castro Propaganda*. Melbourne: Ocean Press, 1999.

Escalante, Fabián. *The Secret War: CIA Covert Operations Against Cuba 1959-62.* Melbourne: Ocean Press, 1995.

Franklin, Jane, "The War Against Cuba," *CovertAction Quarterly*, Fall 1998, pg. 28–33. (CovertAction Publications, 1500 Massachusetts Ave. NW, Washington, DC 20005.)

Furiati, Claudia. *ZR Rifle: The Plot to Kill Kennedy and Castro.* Melbourne: Ocean Press, 1994.

Hinckle, Warren, and William W. Turner. Deadly Secrets: *The CIA-Mafia War Against Castro and the Assassination of J.F.K.* New York: Thunder's Mouth Press, 1992.

Miranda Bravo, Olga. *The U.S.A. Versus Cuba: Nationalizations and Blockade.* Havana: Editorial José Martí, 1996.

Prada, Pedro. *Island Under Siege: The U.S. Blockade of Cuba.* Melbourne: Ocean Press, 1995.

Ricardo, Roger. *Guantánamo: The Bay of Discord.* Melbourne: Ocean Press, 1994.

Smith, Wayne S. *The Closest of Enemies: A Personal and Diplomatic Account of U.S.- Cuban Relations Since 1957.* New York: Norton and Co., 1987.

Cuba and Religion

Bonpane, Blase. *Guerrillas of Peace: Liberation Theology and the Central American Revolution.* Boston: South End Press, 1985.

Castro, Fidel. *Fidel and Religion: Conversations with Frei Betto.* Sydney: Pathfinder Books, 1986.

Davis, J. Merle. *The Cuban Church in a Sugar Economy: A Study of the Economic and Social Basis of the Evangelical Church in Cuba.* New York: International Missionary Council, 1942.

Gómez Treto, Raúl. *The Church and Socialism in Cuba.* Maryknoll, N.Y.: Orbis Books, 1988.

Gonzalez-Wippler, Migene. *Powers of the Orishas: Santería and the Worship of Saints.* New York: Original Publications Co., 1992.

Gutiérrez, Gustavo. *Las Casas: In Search of the Poor of Jesus Christ.* Maryknoll, N.Y.: Orbis Books, 1993.

Kirk, John M. *Between God and the Party: Religion and Politics in Revolutionary Cuba.* Tampa: University Presses of Florida, 1989.

Mitchel, Paul D. *Cuba Calling: A Golden Anniversary Volume.* Buenos Aires: Imprenta Metodista, 1949.

Theology, Ethics, and Jubilee

Brueggeman, Walter. *The Prophetic Imagination.* Philadelphia: Fortress Press, 1978.

———. *A Social Reading of the Old Testament: Prophetic Approaches to Israel's Communal Life.* Minneapolis: Fortress Press, 1994.

Gnuse, Robert. *You Shall Not Steal: Community and Property in the Biblical Tradition.* Maryknoll, N.Y.: Orbis Books, 1985.

Harris, Maria. *Proclaim Jubilee: A Spirituality for the Twenty-First Century*. Louisville, Ken.: Westminster John Knox Press, 1996.

Lancaster, Kathy, *Global Ethics: On the Threshold of a New Millennium*. Louisville, Ken.: Presbyterian Church, USA, Sept./Oct. 1998. (Presbyterian Distribution Service, 100 Witherspoon St., Louisville, KY 40202-1396.)

Meeks, M. Douglas. *God the Economist: The Doctrine of God and Political Economy*. Minneapolis: Fortress Press, 1989.

Rasmussen, Larry L. *Earth Community, Earth Ethics*. Maryknoll, N.Y.: Orbis Books, 1996.

Ringe, Sharon H. *Jesus, Liberation, and the Biblical Jubilee: Images for Ethics and Christology*. Philadelphia: Fortress Press, 1985.

Taylor, John V. *The Primal Vision: Christian Presence and African Religion*. Philadelphia: Fortress Press, 1963.

Yoder, John Howard. *The Politics of Jesus*. Grand Rapids: Eerdmans Publishing Co., 1972.

Ocean Press and Pathfinder Books publications can be ordered from Login Publishers consortium, 1436 W. Randolph St., Chicago, IL 60607. Tel (800) 243-0138. Ordering by telephone with credit card will save several weeks.

PERIODICALS

CubaInfo. Published every three weeks by the Johns Hopkins University Cuba Exchange Program, directed by Wayne Smith, former head of the U.S. Interest Section in Cuba. (Cuba Exchange Program, 1755 Massachusetts Ave. NW, Suite 421, Washington, DC 20036.)

Cuba Update. Published every two months by the Center for Cuban Studies, 124 W. 23rd St., New York, NY 10011. Membership in the center includes the *Update* plus a discount on Cuba books, posters, and other items.

Food First News & Views. Quarterly newsletter of the Food First Institute for Food & Development Policy, 398 60th St., Oakland, CA 94618.

Global Exchanges. Quarterly newsletter of Global Exchange, 2017 Mission St., Suite 303, San Francisco, CA 94110.

Granma International. Weekly newspaper in English sent by air from Havana. (Pathfinder, 410 West St., New York, NY 10014.)

FILMS, VIDEOS, AND CDS

Church and Revolution. Report on the 1997 United Church of Christ Cuba Study Seminar. 70 min. (United Church of Christ Resources. Tel. (800) 325-7061.)

Cuba Calls . . . We Must Answer. Documentary on the U.S. blockade and its impact on the lives of Cubans. 30 min. (Cuba Information Project, 198 Broadway, Room 800, New York, NY 10038.)

Cuba: Three Faith Perspectives.Video on the Protestant churches in Cuba. (See Videography.)

The Cuban Excludables, documentary by Estela Bravo about Marielitos in the U.S. English version. (Document Associates, 1697 Broadway, New York, NY 10019.)

Gay Cuba. Documentary on the treatment of gays and lesbians in Cuba. 57 min. (Frameline, 346 Ninth St., San Francisco, Ca 94103.)

The Greening of Cuba. Film about Cuban farmers and scientists working together to develop sustainable agriculture, produced by the Institute for Food and Development Policy. 38 min. Spanish with English subtitles. (Subterranean Co. P.O. Box 160, Monroe, OR 97456.)

Miami-Havana. Documentary by Estela Bravo about Cuban émigrés in Miami and Cubans who remained in Havana. English version, 52 min. (Document Associates, 1697 Broadway, New York, NY 10019.)

Soy Cubano! Film about the effect of the U.S. blockade on the health of Cuban children, narrated by Alice Walker. In English, 30 min. (Global Exchange, 2017 Mission St., Suite 303, San Francisco, CA 94110.)

Strawberry and Chocolate. Cuban comedy film about David, a heterosexual, politically active Communist, and Diego, an apolitical homosexual devoted to the arts, who become friends. Spanish with English subtitles. 1995, 110 min. (Critics' Choice Video, P.O. 749, Itasca, NY 60143.)

I Am Time. Boxed set of four CDs: Invocations, Songs, Dances, and Jazz (over four hours), plus descriptive booklet. (Center for Cuban Studies, 124 W. 23rd St., New York, NY 10111.)

TRAVEL INFORMATION

Baker, Christopher P. *Cuba Handbook*. Chicago: Moon Publications, 1997.

Stanley, David. *Cuba: A Lonely Planet Survival Kit*. Oakland, Calif.: Lonely Planet Publications, 1997.

Marazul Tours, Tower Plaza, 4199 Park Ave., Weehawken, NJ 07087. Tel. (800) 223-5334.

Study Seminars:

Center for Cuban Studies, 124 W. 23rd St., New York, NY 10111.

Global Exchange, 2017 Mission St., Suite 303, San Francisco, CA 94110.

United Church of Christ Annual Cuba Study Seminar, c/o Ted Braun, P.O. Box, Pleasant Hill, TN 38578. Tel. (931) 277-5135.

HUMANITARIAN AID ORGANIZATIONS

Church World Service, P.O. Box 968, Elkhart, IN 46515. Tel. (800) 297-1516 or (212) 870-3151.

Pastors for Peace, 402 W. 145th St., New York, NY 10031. Tel. (212) 926-5757 or 1607 W. Winnemac Ave., Chicago, IL 60640. Tel. (773) 271-4817.

Send a Piana to Havana, c/o Ben Trehaft, 39 E. 7th St., Apt. 3, New York, NY 10003. Tel. (212) 505-3173.

VIDEOGRAPHY

Prepared by Dave Pomery. All resources listed below are ½" VHS format unless otherwise noted.

PRIMARY RESOURCE

Cuba: Three Faith Perspectives

Sale:	$29.95	1998	28:47 min.
Rental:	$15.00		

During the Batista Years, Cuba was known as the playground of the Western world. Following the Castro-led revolution of 1959, it became a socialist state and the object of sabotage, raids, and a crippling trade embargo imposed by successive U.S. governments.

But what's really going on in Cuba? Is it as oppressive as some people say? How about the churches? Are they really free or they subject to government harassment? This video provides three faith perspectives on the contemporary Cuban reality: Ysel Perez (Methodist), who stayed; Tony Ramos (Baptist), who left, and Carlos Ham-Stanard (Presbyterian), who was only two years old in 1959 and has spent his life as a Christian in revolutionary Cuba.

This documentary lays to rest many myths and raises some significant questions, especially for Christians in North America. Study guide included.

Available for sale only from
    Friendship Press Distribution Office
    P.O. Box 37844
    Cincinnati, OH 45222-0844. (800) 889-5733
Available for rental only from
    Ecufilm
    810 Twelfth Avenue, South
    Nashville, TN 37203. Tel. (800) 251-4091

SECONDARY RESOURCES

Church and Revolution

Sale: $39.95 + 5.00 s&h   1997   66 min.

In 1959 the Cuban revolution transformed a society. With the revolution, churches were forced to reduce their services to communities as the government took over education, health care, and social programs. Many church members left for the United States, while those who stayed behind searched for new ways of living out the life and mission of the church. Despite the challenges, Protestant churches continued to hold worship services and conduct programs that met that needs of people living in their communities. Today, the church works alongside the government in a consolidated effort to address the problems of the country.

Produced by the United Church of Christ, this video takes an historical look at revolution (which the churches were involved with from the beginning) and brings us up to the present day. In 1990 the right to religion became law, and Cuba is seen as a Christian nation. Narrator is the Rev. Ted Braun (author of the study book for this mission education theme). The video is especially helpful orientation for those planning a trip to Cuba.

Available for *sale only* from
> Office of Communication
> United Church of Christ
> 700 Prospect avenue, East
> Cleveland, OH 44115-1100. Tel. 216-736-2201. Fax: 216-736-2223

The Greening of Cuba

Rental: $15.00   1996   38 min.

In Spanish with English subtitles

This video profiles Cuban farmers and scientists working to reinvent a sustainable agriculture, based on ecological principles and local knowledge. In their quest for self-sufficiency, Cubans combine time-tested traditional methods with cutting-edge biotechnology.

Told in the voices of the women and men—the campesinos, researchers, and organic gardeners—who are leading the organic agriculture movement, this video reminds us that developed and developing nations alike can choose a healthier environment and still feed their people.

Produced for the Institute for Food and Development Policy ("Food First").

Available for *sale only* from
> Subterranean Company
> Box 160
> 265 S. Fifth Street
> Monroe, OR 97456. Tel. (800) 274-7826

Map & Facts: Cuba
Oxford Cartographers. Text by Joseph A. Perez

Four-color wall map 23"x 35" showing topography, provinces, and major cities, and Cuba in relation to other Caribbean countries and the U.S. Eight panels on the reverse side provide ready reference to Cuban history, blacks in Cuba, religion in Cuba, relations with the U.S. and USSR, and basic geographic facts.
FP 73028 $8.95

A Child's Glimpse of Cuba
Edited by Martha Bettis Gee

A selection of stories, songs, poems, and games with a short introduction. Available in print and on the NCCC USA web page.
0-377-00327-1 $4.95

CUBA: Three Faith Perspectives
Video, 28:47 minutes

Produced by Berkeley Studios (The United Church of Canada).
Three Christians (Methodist, Baptist, and Presbyterian) inside and outside Cuba, looking at their country from their faith perspectives. This documentary raises some significant questions for U.S. and Canadian Christians. With study guide.
FP 58392 $29.95